WHEN THE VOICES IN MY HEAD FORMED A CHAT GROUP

JUNE BOWSER-BARRETT

Publisher's Information

EBookBakery Books

Author contact: bowserbarrett@hotmail.com

ISBN: 978-1-953080-08-0
© 2020 by June Bowser-Barrett

Author's photo by Ellen Korsch Sargent

ALL RIGHTS RESERVED

No part of this work covered by the copyright herein may be reproduced, transmitted, stored, or used in any form or by any means graphic, electronic, or mechanical, including but not limited to photocopying, scanning, digitizing, taping, Web distribution, information networks, or information storage and retrieval systems, except as permitted by Section 107 or 108 of the 1976 United States Copyright Act, without the prior written permission of the author.

DEDICATION

To my friends and step-children, Shaun and Carolyn, who have been telling me for years to write these stories down!

Contents

FAMILY viii
    Another Christmas Memory 1
    Just a Little Fire 12
    The Great American Cat Escape Caper 16
    Planting Aunt Irene 20
    The Groundhog Advocacy Project 24
    The Paw Print Patio 27

SCHOOL 30
    Fat Ass Breaks Toilet 31
    Nuns 35
    Very Young Teachers 40
    Reservations 44
    The Class: Shakespeare 101- A Dialog 52
    But You Get Summers Off! 61

THE DATING GAMES 64
    Murphy's Law Goes to Lunch 65
    Irish Spring 72
    The Bad Dates Contest 80
    You've Got Messages! 83

TRAVEL TRIUMPHS AND DISASTERS 86
    The Rum Swizzle Inn 87
    The Road's Washed Out 92
    Not So Fine Dining 97
    How to get Along in France 100
    The Moon, the Stars, and Keys 103

FRIENDS 108
    The Housewarming Gift 109
    The House Guest from Hell 114
    Me and the Condo KGB 118
    Monday Night at the Death Café 123
    The Blizzard of 1978 127
    Lunch at the Barnstable County Jail 130
    Chappaquiddick – The Movie 134

Sandstock: The Woodstock Anniversary Concert............140
The Plumbing Plays..146
DANGER! I'VE BEEN THINKING................................150
So, I've Been Thinking 151
What Could Go Wrong? 153
I'll Drink to That!..156
What's Love Got to do With It? 159
Do Not Go Gentle into That Good Night. . ...16=
In Search of the Magic Bullet 164
The Committee...(or How to Get Published in 2019) 167

About the Author 173

ACKNOWLEDGMENTS

Most of these pieces were written under Professor Lee Grove's graduate school tutelage at U MASS Boston and in The Writing Incubator at A.L.L. (The Academy for Lifelong Learning, Barnstable, MA) under the watchful eyes of the coordinators: Wade ("more dialog") Sayer and Nancy (Cape historian) Shoemaker. Many thanks for their feedback and for the comments and suggestions of my fellow (and very talented) writers in that group over the past four years.

Forward

As I've told these stories over the years, I'm always asked, "Did that really happen? Is all that true???" The answer is: of course! . . . mostly. . . well, pretty much! Anyway, I'm an entertainer, not a historian, and as my Irish ancestors would say, "Never let facts get in the way of a good story!"

On the off chance that someone who doesn't know me is reading this book, a little background information might help. I describe my two marriages as being recorded in The Society for Short-lived Phenomena. My first marriage, at twenty-one, lasted four years and produced one child. My second, at fifty-seven, lasted five and a half years until John Barrett died in 2007. I have two step-children from that marriage. So, I was single for thirty-two years in between giving me plenty of time to engage in destructive behavior like winning a bad dates contest. I was also a single mother, a high school English teacher for twenty-five years before moving on to the community college system for another twenty. In between there were lay-offs, a leave of absence, and multiple part-time jobs which, I believe, saved my sanity.

Now, happily retired, I live in Sandwich on Cape Cod where I try very hard not to do anything that could be considered work.

FAMILY

MY FAMILY PUT THE FUN IN DISFUNCTIONAL

Another Christmas Memory

"ARE YOU COMING HOME FOR CHRISTMAS?" my mother asked as the grand finale to the twenty-question quiz that was her weekly phone call.

"Of course, I'm coming home for Christmas. Why wouldn't I be coming home for Christmas?"

"Well, I don't know. What do I know about these modern girls who leave home and go off to live on their own? We send them off to college, and what do they learn? Family's not important anymore; a sense of obligation's not important anymore; how do I know what's important anymore?"

"Mother, this is 1966. Women aren't expected to live at home 'til they get married. We don't want to go from one nest to another," I said with exaggerated patience, this being about the one hundredth time we'd been through all this.

"Nest? Is that what this house was to you? A nest? I suppose now you're going to tell me I was an over-protective mother?"

"No, no. It was a poor choice of words, that's all." If I pursued this course, I'd never get her off the line. "I just meant that independence is important to some people."

"What some people call independence, other people call selfishness."

"Whatever."

"What??"

"Whatever happened to that ad you put in the paper for the room?"

"Oh. I think it's rented. We had this nice boy come over and look at it. Well, I didn't think he'd like it because it was all done in pink and white with all your dolls and ballerina pictures, but he needed a place right away because he's going to the technical institute, and he starts school in a couple of weeks. You've got to hand it to these foreigners. They take advantage of every opportunity they get."

"Foreigner?"

"I think he's from Pakistan or someplace over there. Such a nice boy, very shy and these foreigners, you know, they appreciate family life. They don't need their own apartments and all this wild living. By the way how's what's his name? The one who wears earrings?"

"Earring. It was only one."

"One's enough. Does he borrow your clothes too?"

"Sometimes," I lied maliciously.

"You don't think he's a little. . .?"

"A little what?"

"Well, you know, a little, ah . . ."

"No, I don't know. A little what?" I loved playing dumb. It drove her crazy.

"Oh, never mind," she muttered crossly. "Are you bringing him for Christmas?"

"No, he has plans for the week."

"Oh, good. Well, it's not that I'm glad he's not coming or anything, it's just that your grandmother doesn't understand about men with earrings and pony tails. She gets confused."

☙

It was fifty-eight degrees the day before Christmas. Not only was it not going to be a white Christmas, it would not even be brown. The flabby earth was oozing black mud everywhere. "This is depressing," I said to my cousin Johnny who was driving us back from a cigarette run to the corner store.

"I'll say," he agreed disgustedly, as he drained his last can of beer. "Out of beer and out of bucks. Nothin' worse than being half loaded. Got any money?"

"No, but uncle Jimmy hid a couple of cases in the garage over Thanksgiving. I'll show you where they are." He nodded at me in smug approval. I wasn't his favorite cousin for nothing.

"C'mere, kiddo. Where's my cigarettes?"

"Right here, Nana." Johnny handed her the carton. She was crazy about Johnny. He was supposed to look just like my late grandfather.

"Atta, boy! Now here, you take this money and buy some books for school."

"No, Nana, I can't take your money." I had to hand it to him. He knew how to milk a situation for all it was worth.

"No, you take it. For school. You want to be an accountant, you have to read a lot of books."

"I can't."

"Course you can! What a kid, doesn't smoke, doesn't drink, study, study, study all the time." By this time, she had peeled another ten off the wad in her apron pocket and threw it at him. He caught it before it hit the ground. She beckoned me over and grabbed me by the back of the neck 'til my ear was level with her lips. "Your mother made me this drink. Take it in the dining room and put some whiskey in it, for God's sake. I can't taste anything."

"Okay," I laughed as she stuffed another bill in my skirt pocket.

She grabbed my arm before I could get away. "Do me another favor?"

"Sure, Nana."

"Don't bend over in that skirt. We haven't had a Peeping Tom around here in ten years."

From the liquor cabinet in the dining room, I heard the bell in the front hall. "Oh my God," my mother shrieked. "She's here. Oh, I can't believe it. Come in, darling."

I wandered back into the kitchen and handed Nana her drink. My aunt Helen stopped chopping celery and onions and turned to look. Mother was shepherding a young woman down the hall, squeezing her shoulder and clucking incoherently. Johnny and I exchanged glances. We had no idea who she was. My grandmother was squinting.

"This," my mother announced triumphantly, "is Judy!"

"Who?" my grandmother was still squinting.

"Judy! Louise's Judy," my mother explained in exasperation.

It was beginning to fall into place. Aunt Louise, for whom I was middle-named, had died young. Uncle Mitt, her husband, had re-married a scant six months later. Louise's sisters were convinced that Uncle Mitt was fooling around before he became a widower. Excised from the bosom of the family, he died a few years ago. His second wife died last year, which made Judy an orphan. My mother couldn't resist.

Judy was beginning to look uncomfortable under my grandmother's scrutiny. Her orangey blonde hair was teased a foot high; she was wearing white lipstick, white nail polish, white patent leather boots, and a black leather strip that masqueraded as a skirt.

"Hello, Granny." She held out her hand and continued snapping her gum. My grandmother peered at her intently, and turning to my mother said, "Who does she look like? That's what I'd like to know." My mother was beginning to babble.

"I wanted it to be a surprise for you, Mother. I wasn't sure she could actually make it, so I didn't breathe a word, not a word. Can you imagine? And here she is! Our little Judy, back home where she belongs at last. And, this is your aunt Helen, and your cousin June Louise, and Helen's son, Johnny, and oh, I could just cry!"

Aunt Helen was crying. It probably was the onions, but it could have been her allergies. She's allergic to animals. There was a growl and the sound of scratching at the hall door. The latch gave way, and in bounded a frenetic Great Dane who made straight for Aunt Helen. Even the onions didn't stop his slobbering all over her.

"Get down, Samson, you bad dog. I had to bring him with me. I hope you don't mind. He can stay in the garage or something," Judy explained. Samson abandoned Aunt Helen, crossed to the refrigerator, lifted his leg and christened the Kelvinator. Johnny made a dive for Samson, and the two of us hustled him out to the garage. Johnny was laughing so hard he had the hiccups. We rummaged around and uncovered Uncle Jimmy's stash. Johnny pulled out a church key with his initials on it.

"Oh, man, I am so-o-o-o glad we found these," his words were still staccato. "Can you believe it?"

"I believe it. Tomorrow should be real interesting. Who's coming?"

"My father, Uncle Jimmy, and the boarder in addition to the characters already assembled. Oh, my father's got a rug."

"A what?"

"A rug. A new toupee. He thinks nobody notices. What a riot."

Samson was looking pleadingly, alternately drooling and licking his chops. Johnny reached over and grabbed the saucer to a plant pot, poured some beer into it and put it on the floor for the dog. Samson inhaled it. "Hey, he likes beer," he said in amazement. I wasn't surprised.

I met Ranee, the boarder, at supper that night. Shy he wasn't. After taking my hand and pressing it to his lips while bending over and leering down the front of my dress, he was, fortunately, distracted by Judy. He repeated the performance. Judy giggled and batted her false eyelashes. She was still snapping her gum. She had the fastest jaws in the east.

My grandmother was presiding at the head of the table, considerably mellowed from the afternoon's highballs. "Rainey here's going to be an engineer. Isn't that right, Kiddo? Come on, eat up. You look like you've been living on chicken bones for the last twenty years. Don't they have any real food over there in Packy Stan?"

My mother flashed one of her "I am so mortified" looks at my grandmother who ignored her. Ranee laughed. "Your grandmother is a funny lady," he said to me. "Yeah. She's a riot alright," I agreed ruefully. From the movement of the tablecloth, I could tell Judy and Ranee were playing footsies.

"So, Granny, you going to midnight mass tonight?" asked Judy on a break from toe touching.

"Not me. Bunch of drunks in church at that hour. It's a disgrace. Place smells like a brewery. You kids go for me." She waved away the smoke from the cigarette dangling from the corner of her mouth. My mother coughed.

"Mother, you should give up that vile habit. There's a new report out that says smoking's not good for you."

"I'm seventy-nine years old, and no kid in the government's going to tell me what I can or can't do. Besides, you live 'til you die. Look at your father, never smoked, never drank, dead at forty-five. And your husband, God rest his soul, and your sister Louise, who was a saint!" She looked at me knowingly to drive home the point that I resembled her in name only. Actually, Louise was my middle name. Maybe she forgot. "Yes siree, this may be the last Christmas we're all together." Johnny rolled his eyes. We'd been hearing this for twenty years.

To change the subject, my mother announced, "I think we should all have a little glass of egg nog to usher in the holiday." Johnny and I turned up our noses. We'd been drinking beer in the garage all afternoon. "The kids too. Johnny, I know your mother won't mind. After all, it's Christmas, and there's just a little bit of brandy in it." At that last statement, my grandmother turned up HER nose.

At eleven-thirty, we piled into Johnny's rust bucket Fairlane 500. I was driving; Judy and Ranee were in the back seat breathing heavily already. "What church are we going to?" asked Judy. Johnny and I laughed.

"We're going to the Owl Diner," said Johnny. "Best homemade pie in the city."

"Best coffee too," I added. "Maybe it'll sober you up. You really are getting to be an Alkie."

He was singing "Baby Love" in a falsetto, making the Supremes into a quartet. "Naw. All you'll get is a wide-awake drunk!"

Judy lifted her face out of Ranee's lapels. "But, it's Christmas Eve. Do you think it'll be open?"

"It was last year and the year before. It's open every night 'til three a.m. It'll be open on the day the world ends, for God's sake," slurred Johnny. The diner was a magnet that drew the night people of the city- the entertainers, the pimps, prostitutes, and underworld kingpins. Christmas Eve was an extravaganza.

We returned about one-thirty, extolling the virtues of the choir, the creche, and the congregation. Johnny passed out on the couch. We put Judy in the den, and I ended up bunking in with my mother. She was wound up.

"Isn't that Judy just the sweetest little thing? Oh, I knew your grandmother would be thrilled to see her, just thrilled to death! Best Christmas present she could have had. Did you see how jealous Helen was that she didn't think of it? She seems to be a very intelligent girl, Judy, I mean, not Helen. Don't you think so? And, I think I'm a pretty good judge of character. Not too many people put much over on your old mother. She's pretty hip to what's going on, wouldn't you say?" She poked me. "Wouldn't you say so?"

"Oh, yeah, definitely. 'Hip' is the word I'd use, Mother, no doubt about that."

☙

The house came alive about eight the next morning. I heard banging and swearing and Johnny yelling, "Cut the noise in there." I grabbed a robe and took the stairs three at a time. Nana was in the bathroom, her black orthopedic shoe in her hand.

"Goddam thing. I got it. Makes me sick just to look at it." She gave the "thing" another whack with her shoe. "Spiders. I hate 'em. Always have." I leaned over her shoulder to get a better look at the window sill. There were two half moon strips, fringed in black, a bit skewed now, lying on the white woodwork.

"Nana, that's not a spider. Those are false eyelashes."

"False what?"

"Eyelashes. Look." I picked up one half moon and tried to make it stick to my eyelid. It tickled.

"Yours?"

"No. I think they must be Judy's," I giggled. "Nana, you just killed Judy's eyelashes."

"Well, I never heard of such a thing in all my born days. Seventy-nine years old, and now I've heard everything."

☙

I was picking up the debris from the demolition of the Christmas presents when I heard Johnny calling me from the garage. "Look at this," he wailed in desperation as I opened the side door. There were dented beer cans all over the garage floor, tooth marks puncturing them and little puddles of stale beer spotting the cement. "Samson?" I asked.

"Samson," he nodded. "Look at him." Samson was standing unsteadily by the door with unfocused eyes; he sauntered outside.

"Oh, man, there's only about half a case left. How're we supposed to get through the day on that?"

"You'll manage. Let's get this place cleaned up. It reeks."

We began camouflaging the evidence of Samson's debauchery. My mother shouted from the house, "Johnny, get this dog out of here. He's eating the stuffing." Nana had a habit of setting out the extra, cooked dishes on the porch, so the kitchen wouldn't get so cluttered. Johnny captured Samson while Mother scooped off the top layer of stuffing and threw it away. "Don't mention this to anyone. It'll be perfectly fine. We'll just heat it real good," she said optimistically. I made a mental note to take only the stuffing left in the bird.

The phone rang in the kitchen. I picked it up. "Hello, darlin', this is your favorite uncle."

"Merry Christmas, Uncle Jimmy. When are you coming?" I asked eagerly.

"It's Uncle Jack. Put your grandmother," he said gruffly.

"Oh."

Judy had just gotten up and was on her way out the back door to check on Samson. Minutes later, she was back in a panic. "We have to call a vet. He's sick. Oh my God, what am I going to do?" she moaned helplessly in the middle of the kitchen.

"Who's sick?" my grandmother asked.

"Samson. He's throwing up all over the place, and he's got the shakes, and his eyes are rolled up in his head, and I'm scared," she cried.

My mother's eyes were widening with each utterance. She grabbed my arm and dragged me into the den. "That dog ate the stuffing. What are we going to do? He's poisoned. And it's in the bird. We'll have to throw it away. Everything. We can't have dinner here today." She was breathing in short little gasps, her eyes darting back and forth as she tried to think logically. "How am I going to explain this to your grandmother? What in the name of God could have ruined that stuffing?"

This was something of a dilemma. My arm was beginning to bruise under her grip. Of course, I could just come out and tell her the dog was stinking drunk on the private stash of booze Johnny and I found in the garage, but that would implicate Uncle Jimmy, and he was supposed to be on the wagon. I had to think fast.

"Oh, Mother, I didn't want to mention it before in case it wasn't true, but Samson didn't get sick on your stuffing. I think he drank some anti-freeze in the garage, because the can was punctured and had a leak. I wasn't really sure he had, but now I think that's what happened. It's definitely not the stuffing. I'm sure of it." She looked at me intently, wanting to believe every word.

"Of course," she sighed in relief, "that's it. Of course, there's nothing wrong with the stuffing."

Johnny and I took Judy out to the garage and explained what had happened. The place was getting to be a real sty. "He'll be all right in a day or two, I think, but you better knock off any loud noises," I said. Samson was whimpering softly in the corner. All things considered, Judy was being a pretty good sport about it.

"Kenneth," my grandmother queried at dinner, "what's the matter with your hair? It looks funny. Are you dying your hair, Kenneth?" My Aunt Helen looked stricken. I put my napkin to my mouth.

"No, Nana, of course not," he coughed, visibly embarrassed. There were streaks of bright pink climbing up his neck.

"I'm not your Nana, and there is something definitely different about it." She slammed down her coffee cup. In twenty-five years of marriage, he had not yet resolved the problem of what to call his mother-in-law, and she was not about to help him. He made a desperate attempt to get her off the track.

"Well, Judy, your aunt here tells me that you're a working girl. Is that right?"

"I'm studying for my cosmetologist's license part-time," she piped up, glad to be acknowledged. She was still fluttering her naked eyelids. "But, I work as a masseuse full-time." My uncle's eyebrows shot up.

"That must be very interesting."

"Oh, it is. You really meet a lot of interesting people, you know, and massage is a wonderful way to relax."

"Let's clear the table," my mother suggested. "Maybe someone wants to take a little walk after dinner? We'll have dessert in an hour or so when Jimmy gets here."

Everyone scattered. My aunt shooed Johnny and me out of the kitchen. We stopped by the garage for reinforcements and headed over to the park and the swings. It was another unseasonably warm day. After burying the beer cans in the sandbox, we returned to find the table set for dessert.

"I don't know what's keeping your uncle," my mother said disapprovingly. She always sounded that way when she talked about Uncle Jimmy. It was her conviction that Uncle Jimmy was the reincarnation of grandpa's oldest brother Timmy, who had left Ireland one step ahead of the sheriff.

"Where's Judy and Ranee?" I asked.

"I thought they were with you," volunteered my aunt.

"No, we were in the park."

"Well, I'm sure they'll turn up any minute."

My old room, now Ranee's, was directly over the dining room. There was a strange, rhythmic creaking noise overhead. The hanging lamp over the table began to sway. Johnny and I exchanged glances. Nana pricked up her ears.

"I'm going to ask Jimmy to bleed those radiators in the upstairs bedrooms. They're making noises again. What a racket." Everyone sat very still, eyes fixed on the ceiling.

The racket, which had increased steadily in pace and volume, suddenly climaxed in a crescendo crash. Nobody moved. Johnny and I jumped up simultaneously. "I'll go see what it is, Nana," he said. We took the stairs two at a time.

The old mahogany bed that had witnessed the birth of five children had finally given up the ghost, its bottom half splintered and resting on the floor. Judy and Ranee were a tangled patchwork of sheets and flesh.

"Get dressed, go down the back stairs, and come in the front door," I whispered. "We'll cover for you."

We stepped outside and closed the door.

"What'll we say?" Johnny laughed.

"I don't know. Just tell 'em Ranee left a window open and it blew the door shut. He can always pretend the bed broke later."

"Not totally brilliant, but OK."

"Johnny, look."

"There are lights on in the yard."

We walked to the end of the hall and looked out the window. The garage was strangely illuminated. The back wall of the garage had been splintered in two places by the front fins and dual headlights of a big, shiny black Oldsmobile.

"Oh, no, he's done it again. I better tell 'em." I walked to the top of the stairs and shouted, "Nana, Uncle Jimmy's home. I think he's going to need a little help getting out of the garage."

Judy and Ranee brushed past us in the dim light and scurried down the back stairs.

"Geez, I hope he didn't run over the last of the beer," mused Johnny. "I'm beginning to think that case was cursed."

"Cheer up, kiddo. Remember, this may be the last Christmas we're all together."

He groaned and put his head in his hands. "Maybe. But somehow, I just don't feel that lucky."

Just a Little Fire

FIRST OF ALL, I'M here to tell you there is no such thing as just a "little fire." I know this because I've had first-hand experience with the phenomenon. It all began one sweltering day in August of 2009 when I got a call from my cousin Sandra.

"Hi," she said, "I was wondering if maybe I could use your condo for a week this month. Michael's coming from Wisconsin, and I think he'd love New Hampshire." Michael is the new boyfriend who is boosting Sandra's self-esteem since her messy divorce from Phil.

"Sure," I told her. "No one's using it until the Highland Games in September. When did you want to pick up the key?"

"Umm. Is Saturday morning OK?"

"No problem. I'll be here."

When my husband and I bought the place in 2002, we decided that we would try never to let the place go unoccupied. We rented it out in ski season because we no longer skied, and beyond that, we just wanted people to enjoy it. We had seen too many vacation homes that sat vacant for months, and it seemed such a waste. So, I was happy to let Sandra use it to entertain Michael.

On Tuesday night, the phone rang about eleven o'clock. I didn't answer it because no one who knows me would call at that hour, and I concluded it was a wrong number, or worse, some drunk. Ten minutes later, the phone rang again, and again in another ten. Finally, exasperated, I got out of bed and picked up the receiver. It was Sandra, and she sounded a little shaken.

"Hi, June, I just wanted to let you know that we had a little fire here tonight."

"Oh, that's nice. In the fireplace?"

"Well, no, in the kitchen."

"The kitchen?????"

"Yes, but it's all over now. It was just the stove, nothing else. I think the stove may be ruined. It's out on the deck."

"What happened?"

"Michael knows that I like sweet potato fries, so he had a pan going on the stove, but then he went out on the deck to check the grill, and when he came back in the pan was on fire!"

"How did you get the stove out on the deck?" I am picturing the new hardwood floor scratched beyond repair.

"Oh, we didn't. The Volunteer Fire Department did."

"The Volunteer Fire Department?" How did you know how to call the fire department?"

"We didn't know. The police called them."

"The police?? What were the police doing there?"

"When the fire started, there was so much screaming going on that the neighbors thought it was a domestic assault, and they called the police."

Needless to say, I was not able to go back to sleep and turned on the TV. The next morning, the phone rang at eight a.m.

"Hello, June? This is Ernie Holzman, the property manager for Alpine Village. I guess you heard about the fire in the condo last night."

"Yes, my cousin called, but it was just the stove, and I guess that's out on the deck. It doesn't sound too bad."

"June, the whole first floor is ruined. The fire started in the kitchen. It was a grease fire and they threw water on it which made the flames go up to the ceiling. The cabinets are burned. The fire department had to put out the fire with foam which killed all the electronics in the place, and the smoke damage is terrible. We're looking at about thirty thousand in damages here. I hope you have insurance."

I called the insurance company to give them a heads up, and then I called the rental agency to tell them to take the place off the market. I got Maureen. "Oh, Mrs. Barrett," she said, "I am so sorry about what happened last night." This was before I had told her anything. I asked her how she knew.

"Oh, Mrs. Barrett, you forget what a small town North Woodstock is! My cousin is a volunteer fireman, and my brother is a cop. This is more excitement than we've seen up here in ages!"

On Friday, there was a funeral the whole family was expected to attend. I looked around the church, but there was no sign of Sandra. No one had seen her. It was not possible they were still up at the condo, was it? I called.

"Yes, we're still here. Michael's plane doesn't leave until Tuesday, and he doesn't have any place to stay."

"But, there's a lot of damage, and the insurance adjuster is coming, so I think you should be clearing out."

On Sunday morning, they were still there. I called my friend Linda. "You need to come up to New Hampshire with me."

"Why? You can't get Sparky and the gang to leave?"

"No. They're still there, and I need the place empty when the insurance adjuster gets there. I need moral support."

We arrived Sunday afternoon but couldn't find a place to park. The two spaces allotted to me were filled with cars I didn't recognize. We parked in a guest spot and walked down to number 41. I opened the front door to find Michael, Sandra, her son and his girlfriend, her daughter and baby, her nephew and his girlfriend and her two children. Interesting. The condo only has two bedrooms. I explained that we really need to have the place vacant and why.

"Well," said Michael, "it's your place. If you want us gone, I guess we have to leave." The tone suggested that somehow I was the bad guy in this scenario.

"Can I help anyone pack?" said Linda.

Everyone scattered here and there, picking up clothes and belongings. The other guests carried on with an embarrassed silence, and an absence of eye contact! One by one they made for the door. Michael was the last to leave. He carried a folder which he handed to me.

"What's this?" I asked.

"These are our expenses. The night of the fire we couldn't stay here because there was so much smoke. So, we had to rent a hotel room. And,

Sandra brought up a lot of food that got ruined. We had to eat out all the time because we couldn't use the kitchen."

"You couldn't use the kitchen because you burned it down!" He ignored that comment.

"Here's what you do. You have renter's insurance. Give this to the insurance guy. You'll get reimbursed and then you can pay us. Oh, and there's an invoice for four thousand to pay me for my part in assisting in the cleanup."

"OK, Michael, but there might be a problem with that. You admittedly started the fire, so now you want to collect? It might suggest it wasn't an accident."

"No, there's no problem. I know what I'm talking about. I used to be in the insurance business."

Linda was looking at Michael wide-eyed. "So, Michael, tell me. Did you flunk all your Boy Scout badges or just fire safety?"

The next day we met Tim from Farmer's Insurance. He was very nice, and I must say in retrospect, that Farmer's was absolutely wonderful to deal with. They paid to fix everything except the one or two upgrades I added to the bill. I told him about Michael's wish list.

"June, you do have renters' insurance. Were they renting?"

I told him they were guests. "Well, if they weren't paying to stay here, why do they want to be reimbursed for anything?"

Good question. "As for assisting in the clean-up, we will pay him for that, but that will be four grand less that you'll have for repairs."

Never mind!

It took six months of traveling back and forth to New Hampshire to consult with contractors and suppliers before the place was back in shape again. The kitchen was totally new and beautiful. A year later when I put the place on the market, the family who bought it said they first fell in love with the kitchen. So, all's well that ends well, I guess, especially for Sandra who finally decided to get rid of Michael, a move loudly applauded by the whole family!

The Great American Cat Escape Caper

FOR YEARS NOW, I have had a running argument with my cousin Lily about our differing philosophies regarding the care and well-being of our cats. Lily, along with many – but not all- veterinarians, subscribes to the belief that the world is a very dangerous place, and pets should never be allowed to roam freely in this minefield of modern mayhem. I say the same could be said for humans. We would be considerably safer from disappointments, accidents, and heartbreak if we never left our homes. But, what kind of life would that be? And, can that kind of existence even qualify as a life at all? I visit Lily and her cats – all five of them – and I wonder what crime they might have committed to be permanently under house arrest.

I, on the other hand, have always given my cats the freedom of the great outdoors. I love to watch them practice what they were born to do: sniff, dig, hide, climb, stalk, hunt. So far, there have been no repercussions from this exercise of freedom; they are affectionate, well-adjusted, and not over-weight. Most important of all, they can survive in the great outdoors. The impact of this last statement was deeply imprinted on Lily after the great cat escape episode.

One October day, I got a call from Lily telling me that she had decided to take the family to California for a week's vacation, kind of a last minute stress reducer. "What are you going to do about the cats?" I asked her. I would be the ideal person to cat sit except for the fact that I live twelve miles away.

"I've hired someone to come in everyday to feed them and play with them," she said. I didn't ask how she found this person or who it was, but just wished her a safe trip. A couple of days into the trip, I got a call from Lily. She sounded distraught.

"What are you doing back so soon?" I asked.

"Oh my God! You won't believe what happened. One of the cats knocked out the screen in the little morning room off the kitchen, and they all got out. Kevin, the cat sitter, called me when he discovered it, and I flew back here on the next flight."

"All of you? Jack and Lisa too?" That's Lily's husband and daughter.

"No, they're staying out there for the rest of the week, but I couldn't be there knowing what happened here."

"Have you looked for them?"

"Of course! I found Pitty Pat. She was wandering around in a neighbor's yard." (This was really good news because Pitty Pat has no teeth. They were removed a few years ago due to extreme tooth decay by a cat dentist for a princely sum! Now she can only eat baby food.) "But, there's been no sign of the rest of them. You know they're not used to being outdoors. They're probably freaked out and hiding."

I figured now was probably not a good time to point out that this was another good reason to let the little critters explore the countryside. I also thought that the cats should come home on their own if that's what they wanted to do. If they didn't come home, then that was their choice. What's that saying? "If you love something, set it free, and if it doesn't come back to you, it was never yours in the first place."

Lily had a different plan in mind.

"I'm going to Radio Shack to get surveillance cameras to put up around the neighborhood. Then, I'll put food out under the cameras, and if my cats come in that yard, I'll know where to find them."

Good grief! I love my cats, but surveillance cameras?? I might just opt for waiting until they got good and hungry and came back looking for a meal. A couple of days later, I got a call from Lily.

"You won't believe this," she said indignantly, "but some of my neighbors refused to let me put up cameras in their yards!"

"NO!" I said in as shocked a voice as I could manage. Actually, I did believe it. Who really wants a relative stranger mounting 24/7 surveillance on their property? Sounds like the ultimate invasion of privacy. The really amazing thing is that some of them DID allow her unrestricted access!

When I called her to see how things were going, she was exhausted.

"Why are you exhausted?" I asked.

"Well, every night I come home from work, and I watch all the footage from the video cameras. Then, I have to go all over the neighborhood filling the food dishes. After that, I follow up on the calls that come in from the "missing" posters I put up. By then, it's midnight, and I get up at five a.m.!"

"Any luck?" I tentatively queried.

"I thought I had a lead on Ginger, but it turned out not to be her. The video is kind of grainy, so it's very hard to tell if it's my cat or just one who looks similar. Some lady found a lost cat in her yard and called me. She was sure it was Cleopatra, but it wasn't. But, guess what? When I left for work this morning, Petey was sitting on the back steps waiting to get in. How amazing is that?"

"I guess he got tired of eating the dry food you put in the outside dishes. He was probably looking for his fix of Fancy Feast."

A few days later, kitty number three, whose name I forget, also turned up in the yard. That left just two unaccounted for. Another week passed, and then came a breakthrough. A neighbor's kid reported that he had seen a cat who looked like Charley in a yard a couple of streets over. That night Lily high-tailed it over there to confront the owners for harboring what was definitely her cat Charley. The owners, however, were not forthcoming about surrendering their furry friend.

"This is our cat, Bandit, who's been missing for the past two years. He finally made it home again."

Lily was not buying it. "I found this cat wandering around the neighborhood for several weeks. He was definitely lost and not well cared for. He was not even neutered. I have spent a lot of money at the vet's on this cat. Do you have any proof that he was yours originally?"

Well, the whole family swore that Bandit started life in their household. Attracted by the commotion, a couple of neighbors wandered over to corroborate the story, and before long it was Lily against the word of six adults and three children united in their determination that the cat not leave his happy home. At this point, Lily employed what any clear thinking, thwarted female would do: she broke down sobbing. She later explained it was a combination of frustration, exhaustion, and profound loss concerning Charley's parentage. In any event, it worked.

"Oh, OK," said the dad, "if the cat means that much to you, just take him." The son concurred, and the mother chimed in with: "He was never a friendly cat anyway." No one else in the family spoke up for Charle which just goes to show what a lack of familiarity will do for you! Lily snatched up the cat before they could change their minds, and Charley was back in the bosom of his adopted family once again.

There was, and still is, one cat missing. I think the thrill of freedom and the call of the wild overcame all other practical considerations like food and comfort. The other four are back where they started – under house arrest. And, I still think if there's an open window sometime in the future, Charley is going to find a way back to the home where he was free to come and go. Just saying . . .

Planting Aunt Irene

IT WOULD BE AMAZING if just one holiday could pass in my family without an accompanying dose of drama! We actually got up to December 14th this year without anything untoward happening, but alas a phone call came the next day. It was from my cousin Mark.

"Mary Beth called me this morning. Left a message. Should I call her back?"

The reason for the question is that we have not seen or heard from Mary Beth in low these past 25 years or so. Usually, when we did hear from her, it was because she wanted something, or wanted us to do something no one wanted to do like watch the videos of her father's funeral.

"Well," I ventured, "she probably wants to tell you somebody died. Her mother is like 93 and I know she's been in a nursing home for years. Not that anyone's cared enough to keep us up to date."

"Yeah, that's probably it. So, I should call her back?"

"Sure, why not."

"OK, but something tells me I'm going to regret this. Do you want her phone number, so you can call her?"

"Sorry, Cuz, it's you she reached out to. Ball's in your court."

Now, Mary Beth is a first cousin. Her father was my father's brother. After he died in 1990, we didn't have a lot of contact with my aunt by marriage, Irene, or the two daughters. I last saw Aunt Irene at my wedding in 2001 when she thought I was my cousin Lisa. Her daughters were invited, but ended up being no-shows. Aunt Irene's plus one was her new boyfriend, Tom, and as she kept telling anyone who would listen, "We're just so in love!" I wasn't sure what she saw in Tom, but we all could see what he saw in her. Her dress was low-cut and short-short. She teetered on 3 ½ inch silver high heels. My friends kept asking, "Who is that?" I told them I thought she was one of my husband's relatives.

The next day Cousin Mark called back. "I talked to Mary Beth," he said. "You were right. Aunt Irene died in Worcester. Mary Beth is going to have her cremated and she wants to know if we can put the ashes in the family plot. That way Irene can be buried with her husband. What should I tell her?"

"I don't know, Mark. It's up to your mother. It's her family plot. Grandma Josie bought it before we were born!"

"I did ask her. She wants to know what you think."

"I think it's OK, but Mary Beth should know there's a charge for burying the ashes. My guess is she'll probably forget to reimburse the family."

A few days later, I get a call from my aunt Rose. She is hysterical. "They're stealing from me. I don't want to give away that plot. My mother bought those graves for our family, and Irene is not family! There's only two left. I'm going in one, and she's not going in the other one."

"No, no, Rose. It's only the ashes they want to put in Adam's grave. She's going to be cremated not buried."

"Oh, you haven't heard the latest. Tom, the boyfriend, doesn't want her cremated. He says Irene wanted to be buried. Then some woman, Marie, claiming to be her best friend, called and said Irene didn't want to be cremated, and she should be buried next to her first husband. I never met either one of them and they're trying to guilt me into giving them a spot!"

"This is unbelievable. Of course, you shouldn't be talking to them. Let Mark handle this."

"Mark told them it was OK!"

"What?? No, that can't be right. I'm calling him."

I get my cousin on the phone. "Mark, your mother thinks you gave Irene a plot. Why does she think that?"

"Well, Mary Beth called several times. She was getting battered by Tom and the friend who wanted her buried. She was so upset, I just gave in and told her she could have the spot."

"Why would you do that? Your mother was dead set against it!"

"I didn't want to argue about it. So, what's a cemetery plot?"

"About fifteen hundred dollars."

"The money's not important. That plot was just going to go to waste anyway."

"OK. There are two spots left. Rose is going in one, and I hate to be the one to break this to you, but you have one brother and two sisters and you're all going to die."

"We're all going to be cremated."

"You don't know that. People – relatives change their minds, and it's always good to have a spare in case of an accidental death. There's five grandchildren running around out there."

"No, no. We won't need it. That's silly. It's a waste."

"Yeah, like money in a rainy-day account is a waste- until you need it. But, hey, do what you want."

My aunt called me a day later, still incredibly upset. The other cousins had started weighing in, and no one was comfortable with Mark's decision. Mary Beth was still on the fence about what to do. Meanwhile, it's been ten days since Aunt Irene shook off this mortal coil, and I'm hoping the funeral director has good refrigeration. I finally broke down and called Mary Beth.

"Look, Mary Beth, this is your mother, and you should do what you want with her remains. I have the perfect solution. Suggest to her boyfriend that maybe he would want to be buried with Irene. In which case, he can get a couple of plots for the two of them and they can go off into eternity together. If that's not acceptable, then he'll just have to live with the fact that her ashes will be in the Shawsheen Cemetery with her late husband because my aunt is not going to relinquish that spot."

"Oh," she whimpered, "I guess I could try."

"No, Mary Beth, there's no trying. Be firm. For heaven's sake, Christmas is five days away. You want to have a funeral on the day before Christmas?"

The next day my aunt called to say that Irene's obituary was in the *GLOBE*. The viewing and funeral were on December 24th with burial in the Worcester Cemetery.

"Hallelujah!" I rejoiced. "Well, I guess Tom the boyfriend came through after all."

"It says in the paper that he's her fiancé. He's been upgraded."

"I think that's automatic when you shell out some green for a burial plot!"

"Christmas Eve Day," groaned my aunt. "Will anybody be going?"

"Well, no one from this family. We have a big party on the 24th, and the services are in Worcester. We'd never get back in time."

There was still a little tension in my aunt Rose's house on Christmas Eve. Cousin Mark was testy about the brouhaha he caused in the great burial plot giveaway. Everyone was trying not to allude to the episode. It was definitely the elephant in the room. My cousin Lisa breezed in late as usual, flung her coat on the couch and asked, "So, who's going to go to Aunt Irene's funeral with me?" We all stared for a minute, then my aunt said, "Lisa, it was today. You missed it."

"Oh, no. I really wanted to go."

"Really? Why?"

"I wanted to ask Mary Beth if she'd do DNA testing for me. She's the only cousin I don't have in our data base."

"Well," I suggested, "it might be just simpler to just call her. Hey, we might find out that she's not a relative after all. Stranger things have happened."

My aunt shot me a "that's quite enough look" and we all went back to the homemade eggnog.

The Groundhog Advocacy Project

ALTHOUGH I LIVED IN the city of Lowell for many years, on a 6 or 7 thousand square foot lot, I was oddly surrounded by neighbors with big yards and even bigger gardens – not flower gardens, vegetable gardens. On my left was a Greek family who owned (what else?) a sub and pizza shop in Acton. Much of the produce used in the shop came from that garden in the summer. Occasionally, Chris, the father, would be kind enough to bring me over a big bag of dandelion greens with instructions on how to cook them- Greek style.

On the right side were the Silvas, a very extended Portuguese family, whose garden was the envy of the neighborhood. Every Sunday the whole family of nine children, husbands, wives, and grandchildren would descend on the property for dinner and for helping in the garden afterward. The rows were perfect; there was not a weed in sight. The Silvas never brought me over anything, but that's not surprising considering how many mouths that garden was intended to feed.

We had a very small vegetable garden tucked in a corner of the yard which was my husband's domain. I preferred growing flowers. That was not the only difference in our philosophy of the land. I believe the earth belongs to all God's creatures. So, I had no wish to eliminate the skunks who had lived under my deck for a decade. Every spring, there came marching out the cutest little black and white babies. The family never bothered us or we them. Even the cats managed to coexist peacefully. Often, one of the neighbors would come over to ask did we know there were skunks in our yard? I would very patiently explain that yes, we did, but that we kind of figured it was their home too.

Sometimes, the raccoons got into the shed and feasted on some dry cat food or bird seed. They were cute too. They lived in the chimney of Norman Ross's house around the corner. Norman was a hoarder, and since he could only get into one room after a while, the raccoons were the least of his problems.

Now we come to the groundhogs. I had known about them for a few years ever since they had taken up residence in the yard. Well they tunneled in several places, but party central was under the backyard shed. It was an identifiable family: mother, father (big guy), and babies. They had gotten so used to me being in the yard with them, that they weren't particularly frightened of people. And, that's where the trouble began. Neighbor Chris came over one night to talk to my husband, no doubt figuring he'd get nowhere with me.

"We have to do something about that groundhog of yours who's raiding my garden every night. I have a friend who's an exterminator and he can come over and set up a trap in your yard, if that's OK."

Well, my husband said, "Sure. No problem," and I freaked out. Thinking I was not aware of the laws surrounding trapped animals, he tried to reassure me by saying, "They're just going to re-locate them to the countryside."

"They are not!" I screamed at him. "They have to kill them. They're not allowed to re-locate them. There will be absolutely no traps in this yard, and I will be happy to deliver that news myself."

Chris said that was OK with him, and the next day I saw a trap with some greens in it in back of his garage next to the garden. What to do? If I snuck in and stole the trap, he'd no doubt figure out it was me. I had to find a way to keep the groundhog from going after the bait. Bleach? Well, that smell could be detected easily enough. Vinegar? Same problem. Detergent? Ditto. Cat pea would be great, but my cats were outdoor cats and collection could be problematic. But, I was finally on to something. Urine. Of course! It would be overwhelming to a little groundhog, but a human might not recognize it for what it was.

So, the next morning, just before dawn, I dressed in black and crept into Chris's back yard with my fresh sample. I chose dawn because the family are night owls and they typically don't put out lights until 1 or 2 in the morning. I figured this dose was good until the next rainfall when it might be necessary to repeat the process.

Just as I thought I had things under control, my husband announced that the Silvas had set up a trap similar to Chris's in their garden, and he approved of that measure. "Oh, for heaven's sake," I complained, "do you think the Silvas are going to starve this winter because the groundhogs ate a few tomatoes?" Now, I had a war going on two fronts.

Sneaking into the Silva's back yard was more of a problem. For one, it was wide open and second, they had motion sensor lights. The good thing was their sleeping patterns were the opposite of Chris's family. They retired early and got up early. So, I could go over there after 11 pm, dressed in black, and be undetected. There was again bait in the trap that needed to be treated. I was very nervous the first night, but it got easier as the summer went on.

On days that it rained, I was very busy and drank lots of fluids. A couple of weeks into this diabolical plot to trap groundhogs, Chris was having a conversation with my husband.

"I don't understand it. I've been putting greens in that trap for days now, and not even a nibble. I can't figure it out."

My husband commiserated with him and related the conversation to me.

"Well," I said, "why would they go after anything in the trap when they have a whole garden to choose from?"

"Yeah, that makes sense," he agreed.

The Silvas continued to put bait in the trap through the summer months. By September, they had given up. Chris conceded defeat earlier. A month after setting up the trap, his friend came to take it away.

The following summer, there were no traps in either yard. Both families had made it through the winter with no sign of suffering from food shortages. The gardens went in again, and the groundhogs were healthy. I was sleeping better and free to leave home for more than a few days at a time. And lastly, my husband decided to forego vegetables and plant day lilies. Life was good!

The Paw Print Patio

It was the spring of 2010, and we were in the grip of the worst recession in decades. Bad as it was, I thought, this could actually work to my benefit. How hard could it be in this economic climate to find a repairman willing to do small jobs? Apparently, harder than one might think.

A very bad winter had chewed up the cement on my patio making walking extremely hazardous. Two masons showed up, looked at the job, and promised to return within the week with an estimate. Never saw either of them again. The third mason, Ted, gave me an estimate on the spot and said he could start the next day.

True to his word, Ted showed up the next morning with special new cement made to be water resistant. "Your cats are in the house, right?" he asked.

"No problem," I assured him.

By noon, the patio had a coating of new, off-white cement embellished with "no skid" swirls. Nice.

I was rinsing some dishes at the kitchen sink and talking to my cousin Lisa on the phone when I spotted him. Mr. Martini, the neighbor's cat, was sauntering across the deck heading toward the patio. I screamed, "NO, Mr. Martini, no, no! Stop! Don't!"

I dropped the phone and ran to the door, hoping to head him off at the pass. Not a chance. Fluff ball Martini galloped across the wet cement, then sat in the driveway licking the wet goop off his paws. At sixteen pounds, he had left one and a half inch indentations in his wake.

I called Ted. "I thought you were going to keep your cats indoors?" he reminded me.

"It's not my cat. He lives on the next street," I explained.

"Do you mean to tell me that a cat that's not even yours just ruined the patio," Ted asked incredulously.

"That's about it," I confirmed.

"OK. I'll be right over to fix it."

Just as I was hanging up the phone, I heard banging on the front door. A couple of Lowell's finest officers were outside.

Ma'am, we got a call that you were being threatened by a Mr. Martini. Is the man still here?"

"Oh, my God, it must have been Lisa who called! I'm so sorry officers. Mr. Martini is a cat, and he was about to ruin the cement on my patio, and I was screaming at him to go away, but Lisa didn't know that."

The two officers are looking at me like maybe I really belonged in a group home. "Mind if we have a look around?" they asked.

I took them down the driveway and showed them the pock-marked patio. Ted pulled into the driveway, and all of us were watching as Mr. Martini made another pass across the patio.

Ted said, "You're gonna have to put that cat in the house for the afternoon after I smooth this out."

"We have to catch him first," I whined. We all fanned out across the yard. The officers managed to shoo him into my arms and I deposited him in the family room. After a can of cat food and a nap, Mr. Martini was getting restless. He headed upstairs and I heard him out on the bedroom balcony. Not to worry, I thought. He's not going to jump off the balcony, right? Five minutes later, I heard a loud thud. He did in fact jump off the balcony onto the deck and was now hot-footing it across the newly coated patio. By this time, it was just about dry, and he left a very light set of paw prints.

People ask me if I had the paw prints put in on purpose because they're so cute! I tell them no, definitely not on purpose, and I just hope the next owners of the house, whoever they are, will also think they're charming – but somehow, I doubt it!

June Bowser-Barrett

SCHOOL

HOW DOES ANYONE SURVIVE SCHOOL DAYS?

Fat Ass Breaks Toilet

IN MY ALL-GIRL HIGH school of 400 lovely young ladies in 1960, there really weren't any "bad" kids. We never heard of mean girls, or bullying, or cliques. Somehow we all seemed to know intuitively that life on this planet was a lot better when everyone behaved decently toward one another. So, it still comes as a shock to me to me today when I remember how much trouble we got into at the end of our junior year. By "we," I mean the four amigos who survived freshman hazing week together (yup, it was legal and sanctioned back then). We bonded solidly and felt a loyalty to each other that could not be broken by boyfriends, sudden popularity, or even the nuns.

Ah, yes, the nuns. They were strong women who understood that being strong was pretty much a necessity for surviving this life in any kind of successful fashion. Touchy-feely and concerned about your little psyche, they were not. Most complaints were resolved with "Offer it up to God." If Christian martyrs could endure torture for their faith, then you could certainly suck it up about being sick, cold, hungry, tired, or overworked.

Part of being strong (in nun logic) was the belief that fresh air cleared the mind and fortified the body. We only had twenty minutes for lunch with a mandatory stroll around the yard for fresh air. Inhaling our bag lunches and using the restroom left NO time to go to our lockers and get our coats. We were shooed out into the freezing winter air and told to – "Offer it up.'

One particularly frosty January noon, we decided we just could not face the elements and made a plan to stay in the bathroom until the bell rang. Now, of course the nun on duty knew about this ruse, so she always bent down to scan for feet visible in the stalls. The four of us: Maureen, Patty, Eileen, and I, stood on the rim of the toilet in a bizarre balancing act that required holding on to the sides of the stall while ducking our heads to avoid detection.

Sister came in silently, only the click of rosary beads announcing her presence, and satisfied the place was empty, retreated. But, before we could navigate an exit from our contortions, there was a sickening, ripping sound of pipes escaping from plaster, the cracking of porcelain against a tiled floor, and the whoosh of a geyser of water spraying the stall, us, and flooding the bathroom. Our combined weight had succeeded in pulling the toilet and plumbing about two feet away from the wall.

We were in a jumble on the floor, soaked, freezing, and unable to untangle ourselves enough to find the door handle. Sister opened the door, and in what was probably the closest she ever came to swearing, yelled, "Mother of God! What have you girls done???" Sister ran off in search of Mr. Fitzpatrick, the old custodian, who shut off all the water, effectively nullifying access to the bathroom for the near future.

A few minutes later, we were standing in Sister Superior's office, bedraggled and the antithesis of the young ladies we were supposed to be learning to be. Sister Superior never raised her voice, spoke precisely, and rarely smiled. She was not smiling now and looked at us witheringly over her reading glasses.

"Young ladies, and I use the term exceedingly loosely, in all the years I have been educating young Catholic women, never have I had the occasion to deal with vandalism in any form, never mind on the scale unleashed by the four of you. I am sending you over to the convent where Sister Mary Josephine will give you dry clothes and where you will remain until your parents come to collect you. Naturally, you are suspended and your eventual fate will be decided at a later time. My prayers are with your poor parents who will undoubtedly be devastated by this disobedience and total disregard for property. You are dismissed."

In unison, we replied, "Yes, Sister. Thank you Sister."

For myself, I would have voted to be back in school among hostile teachers rather than at home for three days with my mother who solidified my belief that Banshees were real and did exist outside of Ireland. Our parents were billed for the damage and persuaded Sister Superior to take us back based on the obvious fact that we were more in need of the good sisters' guidance than ever before.

And, that is where the story should have ended, but it didn't. We were now half-way through senior year and praying like never before that some college would find us worthy of admission. Eileen was editor of the yearbook, so we had access to the yearbook room and the photos. One afternoon, Maureen came running up to us and said, "Do you know there's a picture of the broken toilet somebody took last year? Wouldn't it be a riot to put it in the yearbook with the caption 'Fat Ass Breaks Toilet'?" Of course, Eileen would catch the photo when the proof pages came back, have a good laugh herself, and set the original back where it belonged.

That February was a bad year for the flu, and poor Eileen was a casualty. To meet deadlines, Sister Regina Marie volunteered to take over for her. We did not know about this development until the senior class was called down to an assembly in the library. Sister Superior stood sternly, holding what looked like yearbook pages. I felt sweat running down my forehead. She began: "Girls, a most grievous situation has come to my attention. Here at Keith Hall we expect your yearbook to reflect the values and traditions that a Catholic education provides for its young women. Vulgarity has no place in that education, nor does duplicity. The yearbook staff has assured me they had no knowledge of this. I expect the guilty party in my office at the closing bell. You are dismissed." The offending page was left on the table for all to see as we filed out.

We were traumatized. If we owned up to this stunt after last year's debacle, we would kiss graduation, college, and any hope of a social life goodbye. We had to hang tight. Could we do it?

The following morning Sister Superior announced that since no one had come forward to accept responsibility for the prank, all activities for the senior class were suspended until the culprit confessed. We felt pressure from all sides. Three weeks went by. I couldn't eat, focus or sleep without nightmares about getting kicked out of school. Then, it all ended – not with a bang, but a whimper! Sister Superior was not about to concede defeat, but she had pretty much used up all the weapons in her arsenal. Her solution was to very subtly let the incident fade away.

We had done it! We had gotten away with it, and it was torture not being able to tell anyone! Five years later at our first reunion, someone brought up the "Fat Ass Breaks Toilet" caper and asked if anyone ever owned up to it. Maureen, Patty, and I felt it was time to come clean. Most of the girls said they were pretty sure it was us, but they never would have ratted us out. And, that confirmed my faith that I went to school with 400 lovely girls.

Nuns

I'VE HEARD SO MANY Catholic school alumni lately talking about horrible experiences at the hands of "the nuns." It surprises me because not only were my experiences quite good, but so were those of my close friends and classmates who accompanied me through twelve years of parochial school. I attended my 56th high school reunion a couple of weeks ago. We meet every year now having lost about 30% of our class so far. We definitely had stories to tell about the nuns, but they lent themselves to the comedic and light-hearted variety. We remembered Sister Mary Paul who always said, "Excuse me!" when she bumped into the waste paper basket next to her desk. We laughed about the fact that the nuns kept the classrooms very chilly, not as a sacrifice to comfort as they had us believe then, but because most of them were experiencing hot flashes, and it took us decades to figure that out!

I really grew up around nuns. I lived in the very small town of Bedford, Massachusetts, population around three thousand in 1950. It didn't have a kindergarten or a high school at the time, so my father decided I should go to Rose Hawthorne in Concord, a Catholic elementary school with a good reputation for challenging its students. It was a good choice and I thrived in that environment.

There was also a group of missionary nuns who had a Mother House in Bedford, the Maryknoll Sisters. That complex has since become the Bedford campus of Middlesex Community College where I went back to teach many decades later. As a little girl, I spent a lot of time in that beautiful woodsy setting helping the nuns pack for the missions. My mother always took me along when the St. Michael's Sodality ladies worked there. The sisters told wonderful stories of setting up schools and health clinics in Africa and South America, and Asia. I remember my Aunt Lou once said to them, "Sisters, I think it is just so wonderful that you provide all these needed services in so many places and all free of charge." One of the older sisters immediately corrected her. "Oh no, Mrs. Rogers. We always charge whatever they can pay, and sometimes it's only a penny. In our experience, what you pay nothing for has no value to you." That stuck in my mind all these years, and I've come to see the wisdom in it. Free education in America is a wonderful thing, but students (unaware as yet of the tax system) don't appreciate its value because they're not paying for it. My son was a prime example. He always treated school as a wonderful social scene that had academics thrown in as an occasional diversion. However, when he signed up to take an EMT course at Northeastern University, it was a different story. One night he had a bad cold and felt awful. I suggested he take the night off and rest up. "I'm not missing that class," he told me, indignant at the suggestion. "I paid a lot of money for it!"

In 1954, my father died suddenly of a massive heart attack. And, if that were not sorrow enough, Hanscom Air Force Base was expanding and needed more runway space. It was decided that our little neighborhood, comprised of seven houses, would be taken by eminent domain to accommodate the expansion. So, in a Tsunami of unfortunate events, I lost a parent, my home, my neighborhood, my school, and my friends in six short months. My grandmother lived alone in a large house in Lowell, Massachusetts, and that's where we moved. My mother had gone to Sacred Heart elementary school with the Sisters of St. Mary, and that is where she marched me, in April and near the end of the school year – not an auspicious beginning. We were both amazed to find that my fourth- grade teacher was Sister Mary James, the same nun who taught my mother as a second grader. Sister Mary James was a jovial, rotund sister who resembled Mrs. Santa Claus. She was very sweet and never got mad. Sister Mary James took me under her wing and let me become her "helper." She was really my first friend at Sacred Heart and smoothed the way for acceptance by the other kids.

In fifth grade, I met Sister Mildred who was the music teacher and directed the children's choir which sang at the nine o'clock mass on Sunday. One day at practice, she stood in front of me for several minutes. Then she said, "Stay after practice for a few minutes. I want to listen to you sing." I sang scales to get my range; I sang the Kyrie, the Agnus Dei. "I'm going to talk to Father Randall about you," she said. Father Randall was the pastor, and a few days later he called my mother. Knowing that money was tight and my mother was struggling, he chose his words carefully. "Sister Mildred and I feel that your daughter has a wonderful gift, a beautiful singing voice. But, she really needs training to develop her musical talent. There is a voice teacher that we have worked with in the past. Her name is Kathleen Jennings and she would be willing to take your daughter as a pupil. There would be no charge to you, as June would be sharing her gift with the parish."

Miss Jennings then arranged to have me take piano lessons with a colleague of hers. I never did find out who paid for those lessons, but share my gift with the parish, I certainly did. I sang in the children's choir, the adult choir, at the St. Patrick's Day Cabarets, the Christmas pageants, at fund raisers, at weddings and funerals, sometimes at private parties, and I loved every minute of it. I stayed with Miss Jennings for ten years until she died when I was in college.

At the end of eighth grade at Sacred Heart, Father Randall wanted to know which of the parochial high schools in the city I was planning to attend. This had been discussed at home at length, and my mother had decided that I would be perfectly fine at Lowell High School where she and my aunts had gone. I suspect she was a little weary of shelling out money for tuition, uniforms, books, and the sundry other little items not provided in private school. I was a bit embarrassed when I told him I'd be going to Lowell High. He nodded and just said, "I see." Sure enough, a few days later, Father Randall "discovered" that I was eligible for a scholarship at Keith Hall, a Catholic (of course) girls' school taught by the Sisters of St. Joseph.

Keith Hall had 400 girls in total, so it was small and not overwhelming. Every freshman was assigned a big sister, who was a senior, and whose job it was to mentor her little sister through 9th grade. The friends I made at Keith Hall are still my friends to this day, and I am a huge fan of same sex education, especially for middle school and up. The nuns were strict: no talking between classes, no talking in the corridors. We were told to practice self-control, and for 400 giddy teenage girls, that took a lot of practice! We raised our hands to be acknowledged, no shouting out answers, and we had to stand when we spoke in complete sentences. We were encouraged to "think on our feet." We wore neat and clean uniforms, no make-up, no jewelry, and sometimes after summer vacation, we had to convince Sister that the sun had lightened our hair and not something out of a bottle!

The nuns gave us lots of advice. When someone's boyfriend stopped calling, Sister would say, "Girls, boys are like buses. If you miss one, just wait a little while and there's always another one coming down the road." And then there was the famous, "Girls, what you call love, boys call sex!" And, "Don't be too available. Remember, the peach you can't reach is the peach you reach for." We had to show up at the convent before a formal dance with our dates to have our gowns inspected. No sleeveless dresses, skirts below the knees, and no cleavage lower than three fingers below the clavicle. Really, I am not making this up! Modesty in speech and dress was considered a virtue.

Senior year arrived and with it the fever of college applications, but just not in my house. My mother would not entertain the notion of a girl going to college. My father had gone to Northeastern in engineering, but no females on either side had gone beyond high school. My mother's plan for me was to spend one year in secretarial school, get a job, save up for my wedding, and somewhere down the line, marry the boss. "Why on earth would you want to go to college?" she asked. "You're good-looking. You won't have any trouble getting a husband!" Somehow, Sister Ursulita, the school's principal, got wind of this development. She called me into the office one day to ask about my plans after graduation. I reluctantly confided my mother's feelings about higher education. Needless to say, this did not sit well with the nuns. They believed, and we were told often, that when you educate a boy, you educate a man. When you educate a girl, you educate a family. Sister Ursulita said she would have a talk with my mother.

I wasn't at that meeting, and I'm really glad I wasn't, because my mother came home in a fine state of fury. "Who does she think she is, telling me what I'm going to do about my child's education? Oh, you should have heard her! 'We're going to do this, and we're going to do that, and there are scholarships available, and parental support is very important!' The nerve of that woman!" Well, nerve or not, my mother was not about go against the wishes of a nun, and I began the process of applying to colleges. Having one parent deceased, I learned, was a real leg up in the scholarship hierarchy, and I did get a City of Lowell scholarship to four years at U Mass, contingent on my keeping a B average. I told my mother I could get a lot more money if I were an orphan. She failed to see the humor in that observation.

That ended my education with the good sisters, but not my association. One of my best friends from Keith Hall, Maureen Quinn, is now head of the order of the Sisters of St. Mary of Namur, in Belgium. I see her when she comes home once a year and keep promising to visit Belgium one of these years. A few of my close friends are ex-nuns, having left to pursue more rigorous forms of social activism than the Church was comfortable with. Nuns are a disappearing breed. Parochial schools now might have only one sister on staff, and when I taught a course at Rivier College in Nashua, there was only one nun in the English Department, and the president of the college was a man! Sacred Heart School has closed, the building now condos. Keith Hall has become Lowell Catholic and gone co-ed. I suppose some would say, that's progress, but alas, I would not be one of them!

Very Young Teachers

I WAS TALKING TO PAT Cully a few weeks ago about the fact that we were both very young when we started teaching high school kids. She asked me if I was intimidated by them, and I said no, just annoyed at being taken for a student all the time by the staff and administrators and asked to produce a hall pass whenever I walked out of my classroom. My first assignment in 1967 was at Port Hueneme High School in Southern California. Port Hueneme was a Navy CB base and most of my students were Navy "brats" – just an expression. They were really very good kids. Those were the days when there were sixty kids in study hall, and you could hear a pin drop.

By 1970, I was back in Massachusetts, now 25 years old, and quite "experienced" to my way of thinking. So, it was with no trepidation that I accepted a position at a brand new vocational technical high school in Billerica, Massachusetts, Shawsheen Valley Tech. I was told that this school was opening as a "last chance" for many of the area students who had dropped out, flunked out, or were kicked out of their hometown high schools. What I was not prepared for were their ages: the average age of the sophomore class was 19. We started with only freshmen and sophomores and added a class each year. What that meant was by the time the senior prom rolled around, most of the graduating seniors were old enough to drink – legally.

Most of the staff was young too, a fact that drove the gray-haired administrators crazy on most days. This, however, was no problem for the kids; they loved it and treated us mostly like older brothers and sisters. This in turn, dictated how we dealt with them. The absolute wrong approach was one that was heavy-handed or dictatorial. There was no possible way that we were ever going to be tougher than these kids who, we used to joke, chewed nails for breakfast! No, everything was a negotiation.

"OK, guys," I would say, "if you can put these fifteen vocabulary words in sentences correctly, I will read you a very funny story." They loved to be read to. Or, "If you answer the questions at the end of this chapter, you can have the last 10 minutes of class to talk." Sometimes, they were recalcitrant, immovable, outrageous, at which point I would sit down, cross my arms across my chest, look at the ceiling and refuse to have anything to do with them. They hated to be ignored and would promise to be good if I would just come back and be teacher.

This was how discipline was handled. I kept my part of a bargain, and they kept theirs. Neither of us had any wish to involve the administration. It was kind of an unwritten compact that what happened in the classroom, stayed in the classroom.

One fall afternoon, driving home from school, I looked with surprise at my gas gauge. I had only a quarter of a tank of gas. I knew that I had half a tank when I arrived that morning. The next afternoon, I had half a tank again. This seesaw reading went on for about a week. Finally, I went down to automotive and asked the instructor, Jim Mullin, to check my gas gauge. When I picked up the car at the end of the day, he said, "It's fine. I can't find anything wrong with it."

Well, I chalked it up to the temperament of foreign cars and paid no attention to the fluctuations, until one afternoon, I noticed a MacDonald's bag poking out from under the front seat. Further inspection located an empty bag of fries and a straw. Ah ha! Mystery solved! Some kids were taking my car to MacDonald's and probably other fast food spots for lunch. I had a pretty good idea who the culprits might be, and so I rounded up the usual suspects.

"Guys," I told them, "I know you're taking my car and going off campus for lunch every day."

They did not deny it but reasoned that they thought I wouldn't mind because they always put gas in the car. "Look," I explained, "what's happening here is that you are driving a stolen car! I did not give you permission to take it, and I will never give you permission to take it, so if you get stopped by the police or get in an accident, you are felons, and I'm not going to bail you out. Understood?"

Well, they reluctantly promised never to do it again, and I promised not to report them if they kept their word. Of course, they could hot-wire anything, and there was no such thing as a lock they couldn't pick, a skill I took advantage of every time I lost a file cabinet or desk key.

One morning, I drove into the parking lot to find a statue of Ronald MacDonald standing on top of the cafeteria roof. Another morning, one of the huge cows from Hilltop Steakhouse on Route 1 was penned in the office of the Superintendent Director. They couldn't wait to tell me who pulled those pranks, and I never wanted to know because then I'd have to lie if I was questioned. I really got angry at one of their stunts, though. There was a social studies teacher they were not fond of, and he had a wooden leg, the result of a bad skiing accident when he was young. One day they brought in a can filled with termites and let them loose on his desk just before he walked in the room. I wouldn't talk to any of them for a week after I told them what a mean-spirited, unkind thing that was to do.

There was a kid in automotive who always climbed into the back seat of a car and slept until he heard the lunch bell ring. His shop mates got sick of this finally, so one day they put the car he was sleeping in up on the lift. When the bell rang, he opened the door and stepped down about six feet. Miraculously, he was not hurt, probably the result of a totally relaxed body. But, nobody reported it. The point was made.

All of these pranks pretty much paled in comparison to what we now refer to as the "zenith of prankdom." One mild spring day, there was a rumor going around the lunchroom that someone was going to streak at 2:20 p.m., just ten minutes before the end-of-school bell rang. The route was down three corridors, through the library and out the back door to a waiting car. No one really took this too seriously. After all, it was just a rumor. But, at 2:15 there we all were, outside our classrooms, lining the corridors of the supposed route. Arty Thompson, one of the math teachers, was walking up and down shouting: "Popcorn, peanuts, get 'em here before the show starts," and sure enough, five minutes later the show started. A kid in a ski masks and socks, and nothing else, came racing down the hall, careened the corner into the library and vanished in a flash. There was applause and whistles, shouting and, then everyone pretty much just exited the building, not waiting to be dismissed by the bell.

Ordinarily, we, the young faculty, would have been in a lot of trouble for indulging this nonsense and not heading it off at the pass, but it turned out to be even more serious. Our Superintendent-Director, Ben Wolk, was entertaining some hot shots from the department of Voc Ed. in the conference room that had a big window that looked out onto the library. They were drawn to the window by the hordes of very noisy kids lining the corridor, and thus were treated to a birds' eye view of the streaker's sprint to the finish.

The following day, we were called in to the Superintendent's office one at a time and questioned. "Mrs. Bowser," he gravely asked, "what did you know about this incident taking place?"

"Well, sir, I heard some rumors at lunch, but I really didn't pay any attention to them."

"And did you recognize the student running past you?"

"Mr. Wolk," I answered in the most shocked voice I could muster, "of course not! What are you suggesting?"

He thought for a moment about the implications of that question, and for the first time ever, I saw him blush. Very flustered, he dismissed me with, "No, of course not. Thank you for coming in."

The perpetrator of the crime was a senior, Gary Arbing. Those of us who knew that pretended we didn't, and Gary graduated with his class a few months later, with honors, as I recall! My friend Sharon ran into Gary at the Home Depot in Reading a few years back, and we still were laughing about that day. Gary said, "I've never been able to live that down. Every time I connect with someone from Shawsheen Tech, they have to remind me."

I still think it was hoot, although I sometimes wonder if I had lost my job over it would I continue to be so amused?

Reservations

Mid-November

I'M COLLAPSED IN THE cafe, pushing the food around my plate, when I spot them closing in on the booth from three sides like vultures: the hockey coach, the soccer coach, and the director of Phys. Ed. *Some super jock must be flunking English big time this term* I think, as they slide in, uninvited, next to me.

"My, you're looking lovely in that color today," begins Jack in his best snake-oil salesman pitch.

I'm in gray, carefully chosen at 6:00 a.m. to match my mood. I raise one eyebrow. Oblivious, he continues.

"We have a super, huge, enormous favor to ask you."

"Who is it this time?" I ask suspiciously.

"Not who, but what!" Bill jumps in. "This is an offer you can't refuse."

"Wanna bet?"

Sensing I'm underwhelmed by the preceding tactics, Dickie gets to the point. "We need a chaperone for a camping trip to the Blue Hills next month."

I laugh. "So? You don't need me to go play boy scout for the weekend."

"Yes, we do because five girls signed up for the trip, and we can't take them without a female chaperone. Cheryl was supposed to do it, but she just found out her family's throwing her an engagement party, and she had to bail out."

"The lack of commitment among these new staff members is truly appalling," I observe. "No sense of priorities. Go ask somebody else."

"We asked everybody else." Jack's voice now has the edge of a whine to it. This could get interesting. "If you can't do it, we cancel out the girls."

Hmm. I don't like the sound of this. He might have just played his trump card. I wonder if he knows it?

"Next month is Christmas. I'm busy. It's winter for God's sake. Nobody goes camping in December."

"It's a special program. You have to sign up months in advance. We're lucky to get in. Look, it's only three days, Thursday to Saturday. You get two whole days out of this place."

"I lose a day and a half of my weekend. What else do I get?"

"Our wonderful company?"

'Seriously."

"It'll be great. You'll love it. Fresh air, nature, exercise. And we'll all owe you one."

"That's the only thing that sounds appealing so far. Who's going?"

"Good kids. We're only taking really good kids."

"I want names."

The roster as presented seemed reasonable. Unbelievably, I hear myself say "OK." Already second thoughts are popping up like cardboard Santas.

"OK? You'll do it? Great!"

I nod ruefully.

"Oh, by the way, there's no smoking anywhere on the reservation." Dickie tosses this off casually as I'm performing the mid-air feat of refining my smoke rings to perfection. I've recently cut down to a pack and a half a day. My throat seizes up.

"This is a joke, right?" I rasp.

The three shake their heads in unison as the bell rings clearing the room.

Mid-December - Day 1

It's cold, damp, and gray. The exhaust fumes from the bus mingle with the saturated air, misting us with diesel dew. I've packed every sweater I own and am wearing half of them. I have not smoked for six days. Maybe the worst of the withdrawal symptoms are behind me, but I'm still craning my neck to inhale second-hand smoke. I am not a happy camper. My peripheral vision picks up the impression of a six-feet-four kid in non-standard issue E.M.S. gear: black leather jacket, leather hat dangling beads and feathers, engineer boots. Known to the student body as Shaka Zulu, he was NOT on the original list. "He's in your group," I hiss at Jack as I heave my sleeping bag on top of the luggage pile.

The Blue Hills, about fifteen miles south of Boston, are a small, coastal mountain range, the pamphlet tells me. The reservation itself includes over 5700 acres of unspoiled wilderness and was home to the Massachusetts Indians, a branch of the larger Algonquin Tribe. I turn to pass this information on to the kids, but they're fighting over which station to synchronize the six boom boxes they've brought. Maybe later. I spot the WGBH broadcast tower (W-Great Blue Hill, it finally dawns on me), and the ski area sparsely splashed with primary color parkas. Houghton's Pond looks pristine in December; in July, it's almost invisible under the blanket of bodies. Someone opens the gate to an access road winding upward to a place called Chickatawbut Hill. We're the guests of the Audubon Society. Great. Shaka Zulu meets the bird watchers. I start taking notes.

We pull into a collection of sand-colored-cement buildings at the top of the hill that makes Quonset huts look downright homey. Then, we encounter Rick. Very tall, very rugged, heavy-set with a bright red beard, Rick is in charge of Chickatawbut. I'm listening to him, but I'm seeing Paul Bunyon. His voice comes from somewhere under his shoes. It carries easily over a gale wind, shuffling luggage, and the horseplay of fifteen adolescents. Before the bus pulls away, Rick collects the boom boxes, explaining that we've come here to listen to other things. Lots of exchanged glances, but no arguments. No matches, no lighters, no cigarettes. These people are paranoid about fire. Water is scarce and not to be wasted – two-minute showers and shut it off while you brush your teeth.

We stash our gear in the dormitory building and meet on a well-trampled knoll behind the dining hall. The air smells funny. I'm picking up scents of pine and assorted firs along with the muskiness of vegetation long decayed. We are joined by Rick's wife, Janet, tiny, dark-haired and radiating distilled energy. She tells us about lunch which we were all ready for an hour ago. We're splitting up into three groups to learn how to sharpen our sense of smell. Each group will be given a scent: spearmint, banana, or peanut butter. We have to pick up the scent on a trail and follow it until we find our group's flag – green, yellow, or brown. Without the flag, we will not be admitted to the dining hall. Nineteen bodies hit the ground sniffing. Our group has banana. Michelle's looking for yellow snow. "No," Janet tells her, "the scents are colorless." Mud is irrelevant; underbrush is irrelevant, we're hungry and hot on the trail of the elusive banana. Away from the knoll for fifteen minutes, we've lost the trail twice. Laura picks it up in the middle of the hill. We navigate the hill on our backs in the snow, colliding in a giggling pile at the bottom. Triumphantly emerging from a copse adjacent to our landing site is a green flag connected to the raised fist of Shaka Zulu. We stare. Shame galvanizes us into action; back down on all fours, we find our flag draped over a mossy log. Bedraggled, but proud, we gain access to the feast of hot soup and tuna sandwiches.

That afternoon, we're back in the hills trying to make our way noiselessly through the woods, Indian fashion. Fanned out in twenty-feet intervals, every snapped twig explodes like a land mine. Rick calculates that the Iroquois would have had over a hundred chances to capture us in the last hour. Still fanned out, we crouch down for a half hour of silent observation. It's twilight, and the owls are appearing, calling softly. A tangible chill rises wave-like from the snow-covered ground as the last of daylight recedes. There's a stream running under the ice somewhere. We hear it, but it's hidden by the snow, now turned dove gray, with trees and people harmonizing in darker shades and shadows of off-black. A chipmunk scurries over my feet, seeking cover from the ominous owls.

It's hard to shake off the tranquility of the forest. Walking into the brightly lit kitchen, we're a bit disoriented. Lunch was a bonus. We're responsible for our own cooking from here on. We proceed clumsily, but good-naturedly. Rick tells us that most of the owls we saw today are Barred Owls, although there are some Great Horned in the neighborhood. We practice the call of the Barred Owl while the hamburgers sizzle. It's a melodic version of "Who cooks for you?" We get pretty good at it before degenerating into pure silliness.

After supper, we're going out to sharpen our sense of hearing. Janet sends us all back to change our socks. Dry socks are warm. It's perspiration that makes your feet cold. We change socks several times a day after that. It's breathtakingly cold. We walk to a spot about half a mile from the hill. There's a path of sorts. We're blindfolded and sent off one at a time, at three-minute intervals, to find our way "home." Every fifty feet or so, a small chime is attached to a tree limb. That's your only guide. You have to strain to hear it. We wait for our turn tightly huddled together, taking turns in the warm center. I'm not bothered by the dark, but the cold is oppressive. I concentrate on what I hear: the chime, wind, creaking branches, a welcome shout as someone reaches the top. Then, I concentrate on what I don't hear: traffic, horns, radios, TVs, conversation.

We all make it back, stumbling, extra cautious in the blackness. There's hot chocolate and a telescope set up for viewing. I crawl to the dormitory and my sleeping bag. They tell me there's a problem with the heat.

Mid-December - Day 2

I'm cocooned in my sleeping bag, wearing my down jacket because the heat seems to have evaporated, when I hear a loud, sonorous singing voice accompanied by a recorder. I catch a few words of the song. In the hall, Rick's face is eerily lit by a lantern: it's still pitch-black outside. He intones "Ten minutes 'til sunrise. Ten minutes 'til the ceremony of the sun." Janet has stopped playing the recorder. "What?" I ask her.

"Get the kids up and meet us on the knoll in ten minutes."

I know better than to ask if this is a joke. Michelle stands dazed in front of me, hands on her hips. "Are these people crazy or what?"

"I think we'll go with the 'or what' for now. We better get dressed."

On the knoll, flat black relaxes into steel gray. We have formed a circle. Dickie leans over me. "If this is a cloudy day, there won't be a sunrise. That Rick's a ballsy guy to get everybody out here on a chance." We link arms and wait silently. Moments later, we are washed in mauve, then peach, then pink light. When yellow bounces off the center of the knoll, Rick repeats a hymn to the rising sun, part of a ceremony of celebration used in the ancient rituals of the Algonquins. We are drawn to the wholeness of the moment – the ball of light, the roundness of the earth, and our own tiny circle interconnecting with the larger, living organism. A shadowy outline emerges from the tree line. Shaka Zulu has beaten all of us out of bed in pursuit of his own ritual.

We spend the morning hiking with Janet. There are winter plants and evergreens the Native Americans used in teas and medicine. Certain sapling twigs make interesting chewing gum. We gather up armloads of Princess Pine, cones and branches of berry bushes to decorate the dining hall. Thousands of Christmas trees and not a plastic ornament in sight.

The afternoon finds us at the bog. It's a good three- mile hike from the hill, but even under snow there are interesting things to watch. It takes hundreds of years to form a bog, built up layer upon layer, new growth climbing out of last year's decay. We jump on it, and it reacts like a half-frozen sponge. I'm fascinated by some huge, old gnarled tree trunks. "What's their circumference?" Rick asks me. I have no idea. "Put your arms around it," he tells me. They just fit. "How tall are you?" I'm five six. "That's the circumference then," he explains. The measure from finger tip to finger tip with our arms outstretched is roughly the same as our height. He takes out a slender cylindrical boring instrument, drills into the trunk and gives me the sample. I can count the rings back at camp and figure out approximately how old the tree is.

Tonight, we're going rock climbing. The wind has died down, and it's piercingly clear. There's a hill nearby that has a precipitous ascent, but it's virtually flat on top. It was a sacred place for the Indian chiefs and shaman who went there to commune with the Great Spirit Manitou. We have to be quiet because, Rick tells us, there are still powerful spirits hovering there who mustn't be disturbed. It's a tough climb with more than a few skinned shins and chewed ski pants, but once on top, you can see forever. There's a stopped earth stillness; we can hear each other breathe. Boston is a tiny, twinkling North Pole village. The stars seem somehow closer. Even the most blasé among us are visibly impressed. I steal a glance at Shaka standing next to me. He looks like he's come home.

The heat has died in the dormitory building. We move our sleeping bags into the dining hall. We tell jokes, then ghost stories. Numb-tired, I fall asleep.

Mid-December - Day 3

The heat has died in the dining hall. Rick's singing wakes me up and makes me conscious of a weight across my legs. It's Shaka Zulu's head. Laura has burrowed into the bottom part of her sleeping bag, under Michelle's. Our sleeping pattern resembles a litter of pups huddled for warmth, safety – multi-colored lumps soldered together. We are already dressed this morning and arrive early at the knoll to greet the sun. The sky lightens, but the stubborn cloud cover traps the rays. Rick has another hymn handy for when old Sol rises but refuses to shine.

We're starting off after breakfast to follow three different trails into the Blue Hills. Each group has a map and a compass. Most of the kids have taken orienteering. Happily, I hand over our map and compass to Michelle. Lunch is in our backpacks, and we'll meet at Angel Rock around one. There are still a few "Watch Out for Rattlesnakes" signs posted. This is the last refuge of the Eastern Timber rattler, but we believe they're all asleep. We resolve not to wake any. The sky is still heavily overcast. The hills have a bluish-gray tint to them today. When the sun's out, they're bluish-green. A few times, we've picked up a light, musky, skunk-like aroma. It could be a skunk, but it might be a fox also. We're not discerning enough yet to tell the difference. There are several dens of red fox in the hills. We don't see them, but we do startle a couple of white-tailed deer.

Being the last group to arrive at the rock, we're greeted by cheers. Let the picnic begin. It's hard to imagine leaving in a few hours. We seem to be in a different time zone here. We stand up, stretch luxuriously, and watch as the clouds part to let a glorious afternoon sun illuminate Angel Rock. The theme from "Chariots of Fire" fills the air. It's perfect. It's poignant. It's Shaka's Walkman that escaped confiscation. We laugh and stand at attention 'til it's finished.

That night, we're back in "civilization." I'm inhaling bus fumes; some kid's father is leaning on the horn in a fit of impatience. In the snow in front of the building, someone's tramped, in eight- feet high letters: THIS SCHOOL SUCKS. The band, Twisted Sister, screams out of an open car window. I try to pinpoint the odd feeling that's come over me. I succeed. I'm homesick.

Years Later

We returned to Chickatawbut in April, same kids, different program, but that's another whole story. We keep in touch. Shaka Zulu works on the Alaska pipeline. A few years after graduation, Laura married Richie, her soccer coach. They run the Boston Marathon every year. Michelle majored in Biology and works for the EPA. Rick and Janet, in the hierarchy that promotes naturalists, found themselves eventually posted to Sawtooth National Park. We took other groups over the years and enjoyed them all, but there was something magical about that first encounter with the hill. There were powerful spirits on the loose under that winter sky. Massachusetts and Algonquin ghosts breathing into new converts a passion for their land. They succeeded spectacularly.

The Class: Shakespeare 101- A Dialog

Note: *Research shows that most new teachers leave the profession withing five years of their first job. This piece will attempt to make clear the reasons why.*

Mrs. B: Good afternoon, class. Alright, let's settle down. Chatting has come to an end.

(She waits. It is still noisy. Exasperated, she walks to the board and writes in BIG LETTERS: SEX!)

Good. Now that I have your attention, please open your books to page 162, the introduction to the unit on Shakespeare. . . What's the problem over there? Where are your books?

Student: They're not OUR books!

Mrs. B: Yes, I know they're not *your* books. We only have one classroom set. But yesterday we had a book for everyone except Jody and Peter who had to share. So, why are we short three more books today?

Student: The last class stole them!

Mrs. B: Oh, yes, I'm sure English Lit books are really a hot item in the cafeteria black market. Ok. You two and you two share, and in the back. . .

Michelle: I can't share with Brian.

Mrs. B: Why not?

Michelle: We broke up this morning.

Mrs. B: It doesn't matter if you broke up with him this morning. You're just looking at a book. It's not the final episode of "The Bachelor!" Page 162, William Shakespeare, probably one of the greatest writers of all time and certainly the greatest dramatist, was born in England in a small town called Stratford-on-Avon. Stratford was the town, and it was located along the banks of the Avon River. Does anyone know when Shakespeare was born? Peter?

Peter: About a hundred years ago, I think.

Mrs. B: No, before that.

Peter: Maybe during the Civil War.

Mrs. B: The American Civil War?? No. When was the American Civil War?

Peter: About a hundred years ago.

Mrs. B: And when was your teacher born?

Student: About a hundred years ago? Ha Ha!

Mrs. B: OK, this is going nowhere. Shakespeare was born in 1554 in the middle of what century?

Student: The fifteenth!

Mrs. B: No, not the fifteenth. The sixteenth century because we are living in the twenty-first century, but it's 20 . . .

PA System, Voice of Principal Fanning: The bus for the Varsity Football team will be leaving at 1:00 o'clock today instead of 3:00 o'clock, so the driver can be back in time to pick up students at Bliss Elementary. The bus company is short a bus and a driver. Please excuse the inconvenience.

Mrs. B: Wait! Wait! We have four varsity players, and where are you girls going?

Students: We're cheerleaders!

Mrs. B: Well, OK, but since you're going to miss class AGAIN, please read pages 162 through 183 for tomorrow.

Students: We can't. We don't have books!

Mrs. B: Right. Yes, Amy, what is it?

Amy: Mrs. B, are you going to erase that word SEX off the board?

Mrs. B: Why, does it bother you?

Amy: Pastor wouldn't like it.

The Class: Shakespeare 101 - A Dialog

Mrs. B: Your pastor wouldn't like it? OK, we will now obliterate all traces of sex from this classroom. Oh, I didn't see this. It's a note from the office.

> "Mrs. B, please admit a new student, Mike Hunt, to your sixth period English class. Thank you,
> Mrs. DeFelice."

Hmmm. Is there a new student in class? Mike Hunt? Where is Mike Hunt? Is Mike Hunt here? What is so funny? Is something funny, young man? Would you like to stand up and tell us what is so amusing?

Student: No, nothing funny!

Mrs. B: No? Then, I suggest you stop that nonsense and get busy reading. Hmm. This note doesn't look like Mrs. DeFelice's writing. I'll have to check on this later. Yes, John?

John: I have to go to the can, man.

Mrs. B: "I have to go to the can, man," is not a legitimate request to be excused. No, put your hand down. You just came back from lunch break AND you spend fifteen minutes out of class everyday wandering around somewhere. *Hand. Down.*

PA System - Voice of Principal Fanning: Excuse the interruption. This is a reminder to all students and staff that the DARE assembly scheduled for last Wednesday will be held tomorrow morning during fourth period. If you have a scheduled study period during that time, you are required to report to the assembly. If fourth period is your scheduled lunch, please pick up a bag lunch from the cafeteria on your way to your fifth period class. Since there is no eating or drinking allowed in classrooms, lunches must be consumed before entering the room. Failure to comply with these directions will result in disciplinary action. That is all. Thank you.

Mrs. B: Now, class, to return to our discussion of William Shakespeare, there has been a raging controversy over the years as to who actually wrote Shakespeare's plays. Some scholars argue that since Shakespeare came from a small village and had only a sixth grade education, it was unlikely that he could have produced such masterpieces as JULIUS CAESAR or ANTONY AND CLEOPATRA. Other scholars argue that... where are you boys going?

Students: A SADD meeting today.

Mrs. B: A meeting of SADD? Students Against Drunk Driving? I have it on the best authority that you three are the biggest drinkers in the senior class.

Students: No, Mrs. B, we don't drink anymore.

Mrs. B: That's right. You don't drink any more than you did last week. Sit down. You're not going anywhere. Put your hand down, John. You're not going to the can, um, bathroom either. So, Shakespeare's plays might possibly have been written by someone other than the Bard himself, and the most likely candidate is a nobleman named Edward de Vere, the 17th Earl of Oxford. This person would have had a first-class education, traveled extensively, spent time at the court of Queen Elizabeth and King James... What?? You're passing notes? If I'm talking, you should be TAKING notes. Give me that. "To Brain." Brain? Who is Brain?

Student: No, not Brain. It's BRIAN.

Mrs. B: OK, well, he probably can't spell your name either. Let's file this in the wastebasket. Shakespeare was an actor before he was a playwright, and in the 16th century, that meant something very different from what it means today. Acting was considered a very low status occupation. Yes, a question?

Student: Why are we studying dead guys from a hundred years ago?

Mrs. B: Actually, it's more like four hundred years ago, and the reason is that the works are masterpieces, and all *educated* people have a knowledge of great literature. Michelle, there is no texting in class. You know the rules. Give me that phone... What? You're going to sue me? For taking your phone? Sure. Take a number. I think we're up around 36 by now.

Michelle: Oh, I can't believe what a bitch you are!

Mrs. B: I am such a bitch?? Well, that's the first accurate statement you've made in class so far! And, by the way, you have no idea what a bitch

The Class: Shakespeare 101 - A Dialog

I can be! So, back to our subject. Some people think Shakespeare began writing plays so he could get better roles as an actor. If the plays were really written by the 17th Earl of Oxford, he would not have been able to admit that he was involved in the theater. His family would have disowned him. Cut him off from all the money. Couldn't have that. What is it, Amy?

Amy: Mrs. B, your earrings look like witchcraft symbols. Pastor showed us some symbols in Sunday school last week that look a lot like those.

Mrs. B: No, Amy, they are definitely NOT witchcraft symbols! Take a closer look. He went to Jared's not Salem. So, the first play we're going to read is ROMEO AND JULIET. It's a story you should be able to relate to because the two main characters are even younger that you are when they meet, fall in love, and marry, all in the space of a couple of days.

Student: If we saw the movie, do we still have to read it?

Mrs. B: Well, unfortunately for you, the test will be on Shakespeare's words and not Hollywood's script. But, certainly. Watching the movie is a good place to start. Peter?

Peter: You look very nice today, Mrs. B. Have you lost weight?

Mrs. B: Thank you, Peter, I'm glad you think I look nice today, but no, I haven't lost weight. However, you definitely get points for giving that compliment.

John: I think you look like a friggin' bone rack, Mrs. B. How many points do I get for that? And, can I go to the can??

Mrs. B: No, John you do not get any points for that. It does not qualify as a compliment, and, no, you can't go to the can!

PA SYSTEM - VOICE OF PRINCIPAL FANNING: Attention students. We have a situation here that I consider to be very serious. It is an act of vandalism that will not be tolerated. Someone, or several someones, knocked down the tree in the courtyard that was a gift to the school from the class of 2008. We will find out who you are, and we will apply the full force of the law against you for such willful, vicious destruction of property. You cannot run. You cannot hide. We will find you. Be afraid. Be very afraid.

Mrs. B: I know. That is pretty funny. Mr. Fanning is the only one in the building who doesn't know that the custodian knocked down the tree backing up on the riding mower. Yes, it was fun to watch. I wonder who's going to tell him?

PA SYSTEM - VOICE OF PRINCIPAL FANNING: Attention students. Please disregard the previous announcement. That is all.

Mrs. B: Case close! Oh, before I forget, let me return your essays on a favorite place you visited. Although, I have one that puzzles me – especially the title: "Sinners at lake Cannabis." Michelle, would you like to explain the title?

Michelle: It's "Seniors at Lake Canobie."

Mrs. B: But, that's not what it says. It's spelled wrong.

Michelle: It can't be spelled wrong. I put it through spell check.

Mrs. B: Well, class that brings up a very good point. Spell check won't pick up on the fact that you used the wrong word if it's spelled correctly. Now, I found a little poem that illustrates that point. Please take a look at this. Pass it back please.

The Spell Checker Poem

*Eye have a spelling chequer
It came with my pea sea
It plainly marques four my revue
Miss steaks eye kin knot sea.*

*Eye strike a key and type a word
And weight four it two say
Weather eye am wrong oar write
It shows me strait a weigh.*

*As soon as a mist ache is maid
It nose bee fore two long
And eye can put the error rite
Its rare lea ever wrong.*

*Eye have run this poem threw it
I am shore your pleased two no
Its letter perfect awl the weigh
My chequer tolled me sew!*

∼

(*A 1993 candidate for a Pullet Surprise in Poetry*)

Mrs. B: Yes, Amy, what is it?

Amy: Mrs. B, pastor would like to know what you think of the new Gay and Lesbian Rainbow Coalition Club at the school?

Mrs. B: Hmm. Well, Amy, you can tell pastor that we think all God's children have a place in the choir.

Amy: What does that mean, Mrs. B?

Mrs. B: Pastor will know what it means. Now, who can find the errors in the first two lines of the poem? Anyone? O.K. Try lines 3 and 4.

Student: It looks fine to me!

Mrs. B: Well, it's not fine! And, for your homework you will return a corrected copy to me tomorrow.

Student: Hey, Mrs. B, that's a lot of work.

Mrs. B: No, it's NOT a lot of work. When I was your age, we were expected to do a minimum of three hours of homework a night. Of course, that was a long time ago – shortly after the Civil War. By the way, when was the Civil War?

Student: About a hundred years ago.

Mrs. B: No, but you're getting closer. What is it John?

John: You look hot in that outfit, Mrs. B.

Mrs. B: Alright, John, for your information, I am too old and too tired to look "hot" in anything, and no, you cannot go to the can! Put your hand down! What is this writing on this desk? "Mrs. B sucks donkey balls." Oh! You are in big trouble young man.

Student: I didn't write that. It wasn't me.

Mrs. B: You didn't write it? Well, for your information, I check every desk before class every day, and that does not bode well for you. . . . I can do WHAT to myself? No thank you, young man, and DO NOT extend that invitation a second time. OUT! John! Sit down, John. John! Close that window.

Amy: Mrs. B: He's peeing . . . Look!

Mrs. B: Yes, Amy, I know that he is peeing out the window. I am NOT looking because if someone asks me if I saw it, I want to be able to say no.

Amy: Mrs. B, I'm not sure that pastor would approve of your teaching methods.

Mrs. B: Tell pastor that if he wants to discuss my teaching methods, he'll have to GET IN LINE!

PA System - Voice of Principal Fanning: Please heed the fire alarm, and walk to the nearest exit in an orderly fashion. Remain outside until the all clear signal is sounded. Thank you.

Mrs. B: AHHHHH! I give up!

But You Get Summers Off!

IT NEVER FAILS. I know what the line is before they open their mouths. Anytime a teacher complains about the least little thing, the response is always a shrug and a, "Yeah, but you get summers off!" I could tell them that I don't get summers off; that my meager salary makes it necessary to teach summer school, tutor, work as a camp counselor, a life guard; that the state of Massachusetts makes me go to seminars and take classes in the summer to keep up my certification; that I need to come up with a new course every summer complete with texts and lesson plans; that I'm lucky if I get one week off in the midst of all this so-called "free time." I can tell by the look on their faces that they patently do not believe me.

I can quote them the statistic that most new teachers leave the profession after three years, discouraged by the amount of work relative to the amount of compensation, tired of being bullied by parents who just want good grades without the component of good effort; exhausted from the extra-curricular responsibilities which tend to be compensated at pennies per hour: year book, class advisor, PTA liaison, sports coach, club advisor, newspaper, etc., etc., etc. They would look at me and say, "Yeah, but you get summers off!"

And if I told them the number of teachers that are assaulted every year by students and sometimes by parents, and that now some school districts want teachers armed, or that in one school district in Indiana teachers were injured in a training session using pellet guns to simulate an active shooter situation, or that school have become dangerous places where we NEED to train for active shooter situations, they would let that sink in for a moment and then say, "Yeah, but you get summers off!"

The buildings aren't air-conditioned. There was some talk of calling off school when the temperature went above 90 degrees, but that came to nothing. Ever try to teach twenty-five sweating, grumpy kids, heads on desks, just thinking about an escape from captivity? In the winter, the heat can go out. The lavatories leak, the paint peels, and the cafeteria is about as sanitary as a bus station. From middle school up, the kids are sleep deprived. They go to bed late and get up early. They can't read for more than ten minutes without nodding off. Concentration? Forget about it. If you consume enough Starbucks or Red Bull you can be alert, but it certainly wreaks havoc on the nervous system, resulting in acting out and hyper-activity. And yet, it is my job to motivate, monitor, and mentor without any viable support system in place. Does that sound like fun? "Yeah, but you get summers off!"

And if I mentioned that layoffs are a seasonal malady brought on by budget cuts, poor planning, and a fair amount of waste, or that no administrator is ever going to get the axe, and that the school committee is basically a stepping stone to higher political office, and that the last people ever consulted about policy changes are the teachers charged with implementing them, and that my neighbors act like I'm taking bread off their table if I get a 2% raise, people would listen, and nod their heads before they came up with, "Yeah, but you get summers off!"

Sunday nights when everyone is watching *Downton Abbey*, or *March Madness* basketball, I'm doing lesson plans, correcting papers, writing recommendations for private high schools or colleges, emailing make-up test reminders, soothing a frantic parent who tells me her kid "just can't fail!" I haven't done any reading for pleasure in months; I barely have time to skim the newspaper. Monday morning, I watch with envy as my neighbors walk to their cars unencumbered. I am balancing three textbooks, a bulging briefcase, my purse, a big Manila envelope of potential prom sites, and my lunch (the cafeteria having been previously discussed). I will return home similarly burdened after an afternoon faculty meeting, a prom committee meeting, and a parental teleconference with all of the kid's five teachers. I can say I'm exhausted, but what weight does that carry when after all, "You get summers off!"

I've had fantasies of telling the principal what he can do with his lame evaluations; of telling the school committee they have my vote only if they run for dog catcher; of telling parents that the real problem is that the apple doesn't fall far from the tree, but that would very likely get me fired. Then, I would have to find another job in another field where I definitely would not get the summer off!

THE DATING GAMES

Murphy's Law Goes to Lunch

IT WAS DURING ONE of those years when I went through two or three jobs trying to match my rather esoteric talents to the narrow confines of corporate job descriptions that I first collided with Allen. It was my second day at the agency, and I was still trying to recover from the shock of what a pit the place really was. I had interviewed in the VIP suite on the second floor, a trendy, expensive sanctuary resplendent with track lighting, potted palms, oriental rugs, and enough paneling to defoliate the White Mountains National Forest. I thought, "I've come home at last," when they offered me the job. The agency was Boston's second largest charter travel company, and I guess the bargain prices depended on keeping a limbo-low overhead. Still, gray concrete floors, brown pegboard cubbies, and rusting steel beam ceilings did seem to be carrying austerity to an extreme.

I was just giving myself the lecture about when life gives you lemons, make lemonade when Allen appeared next to my desk and strained over my shoulder to see what I was working on. I didn't even say hello because I was too busy looking for something to blot up the coffee he had trickled on to a stack of papers as he was leaning over my shoulder.

"No, no, I'm sorry. I'll get something. You stay right where you are." He disappeared around the partition and returned with a box of tissues, commandeered, no doubt from some unsuspecting secretary on break. I stood up and reached for a tissue at the same time he reached down to mop up the mess and took a direct hit on the nose from his forehead. Now I really needed the tissues. I lost a lot of mascara in the encounter!

"You know," he observed, peering into my eyes, "you're a very pretty girl. Are you Jewish?"

"Actually, I'm not," I sniffled. "Why do you ask?"

"I'm supposed to be looking for a nice Jewish girl to marry. I haven't had much luck so far, but I've had a lot of fun dating girls who aren't Jewish and who aren't 'nice' in the way my mother would define it. Now see, I wouldn't take you out because while you are very attractive, you seem to be 'nice' in the old-fashioned sense of the word, and that's not what I'm into this year."

For a full ten seconds, I looked at him steadily and in my most condescending voice said, "Thank you for sharing that with me." Oblivious to the put-down, he picked up the box of tissues, muttered something about having work to do and knocked the plant off my desk as he turned to leave.

"Don't!" I said before he could touch anything. "Just keep walking. Don't stop. Don't say anything!" Over his shoulder, he gave me that I-was-only-trying-to-help-look and almost walked into a partition.

I thought maybe he was well known as the office character and decided to ask around. I was told that he was only a little more senior than I was at the job and that he had come highly recommended from another agency. Beyond that, there was no gossip, no scandal, nothing. The following week, we were both assigned to the same project. Allen seemed genuinely pleased with this arrangement, came up with a lot of creative suggestions and spent the rest of the time lampooning the rather limited talents of our project director. I was becoming convinced of what I had already begun to suspect- working with Allen was going to be fun – a little zany and eccentric, but fun.

Days passed with nothing more disquieting than Allen locking my file cabinet before I could tell him there was no key. In the midst of trying to straighten out that mess, he said suddenly (as if it were the most original thought he'd ever had) "Why don't we go out and have lunch? It's pretty quiet around here today, and we've been working too hard anyway. I'll take you over to Brookline to my old neighborhood. You're going to love this Deli. It's fantastic. What do you say?"

I said "yes" first, because I was starving and second because I would have felt guilty squelching that kind of enthusiasm.

"We'll take my car," he volunteered. "It's new. A BMW. You probably drive an Escort."

"I don't." I bristled, "but the point I was going to make is that we should take the 'T'; you might not get your parking space back this afternoon."

"No problem," he bragged. "I'm tight with the guard."

The Deli was, as he has promised, a terrific place. It was a little more upscale than I imagined a Deli would be, with white table cloths, bud vases with fresh flowers and tiny candle lanterns. It was also incredibly crowded and took an age and a half to get served. By this time, the better part of an hour had gone by, and I started to get a little nervous about taking so long for lunch. "Don't worry about it," he said. "It's not like we do this everyday, and besides we'll be back in half an hour. Nobody's keeping tabs on us, I'm sure."

At the end of the next half hour, we asked for our check. Fifteen minutes later, it arrived.

"Let me split it with you," I insisted.

"Absolutely not," he said indignantly. "I invited you to lunch."

"Well, you suggested which restaurant to go to, but I didn't really think of it as you taking me to lunch. Really, let me split it with you."

With that, he bolted up out of his chair announcing, "Too late. I've got it and you can't get it!" What he didn't notice was that with the check his fingers had caught a corner of the table cloth and in one long stride up the aisle, he managed to remove the table cloth, the dishes and silverware along with a vase of flowers and assorted condiments. The lantern was still glowing reassuringly on its original spot.

From every corner of the restaurant, waiters converged, fumbling in their eagerness to restore the place to some kind of order. All of this provided great entertainment for the lunch crowd. I was hoping against hope that Allen wouldn't try to assist the waiters in cleaning up the mess. Apologizing profusely, we slunk down the aisle to the cashier.

Escaping into the sunshine and fresh air, I started to giggle.

"Are you going to start laughing at me?" he asked in a hurt voice.

"I'm not laughing at you. I'm just thinking about the situation and appreciating the humor in it."

"Oh, sure. I know. You were laughing at me. But that's O.K. I'll get over it. I always do."

"If you're going to go melodramatic on me, I'm taking the 'T' back."

"I promise to be good. Do you have my car keys?"

"Why would I have your car keys?"

"Because they're not in my pockets and I figured I gave them to you."

"Well, I don't have them. You don't suppose you locked them in the car, do you?"

"No, of course not. Do you see any keys in there?"

"No. Maybe you dropped them somewhere. We can take the 'T' back."

"No need. I always keep an extra set on a magnet under the rear fender. All I have to do is reach under here and pull them out."

As he was reaching under the car, a wave of panic swept over his face.

"They're not there?" I asked tentatively.

"Well, I can't seem to reach them from here. I'll have to go under the car and look."

"You can't go under the car! The street's all mud. There's half a foot of snow melting. We'll take the 'T'."

Before I could finish the last sentence, he was under the car in his tan raincoat and Khaki pants.

"Did you find it?" I asked, after about a minute had gone by.

"There's not enough light to see anything under there. But that's not the problem. I'm caught."

"Caught? What do you mean 'caught'? Caught on what?"

"If I knew that I wouldn't be stuck. My raincoat's caught on something, and I can't get it loose."

"No, there's not enough room." Several seconds ticked by unproductively.

"Allen, you cannot stay under that car indefinitely. I'm going to crawl under and help you."

"No, don't do that. You'll get filthy."

"Tell me about it. We have to get out of here."

As I got down on my knees to inch my way under this small foreign car, I kept telling myself, "I can't believe I'm doing this."

It was now way beyond any decent interval for lunch. In fact, it was after 2:30 p.m. We had been gone over two and a half hours. Great show for two new employees.

"I see what you're caught on. I'll try to ease it off this hook or whatever it is." I tugged gently; it wouldn't budge. I gave it a good yank and heard a ripping sound as the raincoat separated itself from the vehicle. "You're free, Allen. Now, be careful getting out of here. There's not much room."

I slowly inched my way out from under the car, feeling the damp pavement soaking into my thighs. This could only mean that my skirt was hiked up about half-way to my waist. Pushing with one hand and trying to pull my skirt down with the other, I emerged to a pair of heavy black shoes and dark blue trousers. They looked familiar.

"Oh, hello, officer. We're locked out of the car." He was looking at me strangely. At the word "Officer," Allen slid forward, feet first and whacked his head on the bumper on the way up. There was a trickle of blood running down his cheek. He was soaked through with mud on his backside, and the front of him was smeared with grease.

"Oh my God, look at you. You're a sight," I groaned.

"Yeah? Take a look at yourself."

I was a clone, minus the blood running down my cheek. We had to convince the officer that it was really Allen's car and that we weren't two derelicts up to no good. In our present get-ups, it took some doing.

"What time is it?" I could feel the beginning of a small knot coiling in my stomach.

"It's three o'clock. Let's get a cab back. I have a spare set of keys at home, and the building super can let me in."

This time I made no fuss as I did not wish to be observed in this condition by the ridership of the public transit system. Allen, after several unsuccessful attempts, finally flagged down a cabbie, and we got in. I looked at him and started to laugh. I couldn't stop. It was really too ridiculous. The cabbie wanted to know what was so funny and since I couldn't talk, Allen started filling him in on the afternoon's misadventures. The cabbie laughed 'til his glasses fogged up, and I guess that's why he didn't see the guy who was running the red light. There was a thudding crunch of metal and the tinkling of glass. Silence. The cabbie jumped out and opened the back door.

"You folks all right?" he asked, kind of shaky. I couldn't answer him because I was laughing even harder. I had to find a bathroom fast. I started off down the street at a trot. Allen came running after me. He was babbling about staying as a witness, but I just waved my hand to show I couldn't care less. We were only about a block from the office.

"OK, OK, now," Allen looked serious. "You have to promise me you will not, I mean will NOT tell anyone what happened this afternoon. Promise me."

"Allen, for God's sake, how are we going to explain walking in three hours late looking like this? Course we have to tell them."

"We have to tell them SOMETHING, but not that. Look, I've got it. We'll say we were mugged. Why not? We look like we were mugged. And you, I'll say they tried to attack you, and I fought them off, and that's how I got this," he pointed to his forehead. "OK??"

"I can't tell them that. If you want to tell them that, go ahead. I can't just make all that stuff up."

"OK, I'll tell the story. You just nod."

"OK," I agreed, as the elevator door opened into our work area. We walked off the elevator, and people sort of wandered away from their desks to stand and stare at us. Nobody said anything. Finally, Ruth, Allen's supervisor, broke the spell.

"Where the hell did you two go for lunch? A war zone?"

"Ruth! We could've been killed. We were attacked. Robbed!"

As I stood there listening to Allen fabricate his tale of urban trauma and terror, I could feel myself losing control; I always laugh when things are really tense. Nervous reaction. The more I tried to suppress it, the less control I had until finally I was standing there howling. At this point, the crowd looked definitely confused. I turned around, walked to the elevator and went home.

The next day, Allen was sticking to his story. I kept my promise to Allen and never told what really happened ('til now), but I never elaborated on the story either. It turned into the biggest mystery and source of office gossip that International Weekends, Inc. had ever experienced.

Allen became a good and loyal friend, and I saw him from time to time even long after I left the agency. As truly fond of him as I am, I never went out to lunch with him again unless we had a chaperone or two to keep things sane. And, he's still looking for a nice Jewish girl to marry. For her sake, I sort of hope he never finds her.

Irish Spring

SO, IT'S ST. PATRICK'S Day, and I'm in Dublin. I'm just finishing up breakfast at Jury's on Custom House Quay. This is not a small task since I'm coming off an overnight, red-eye flight, during which I got about seven minutes of sleep, and the previous day, my first full day in Ireland, I spent at the Guinness Brewery at St. James Gate on no sleep at all.

Now ordinarily a tour of the Guinness Brewery would be a rather boring look at seven floors of vats, copper holding tanks, tubes, hoses and the like, but this is March 16th, and the city is in a party mood. My cousin and I figure out that not only is there a bar on the 7th floor which boasts 360 degree views of the city, but there is a LIVE BAND and a cash bar set up on each one of the SEVEN floors!

It becomes our mission to have a pint on each floor because The Book of Kells, after all, isn't going anywhere and will most likely be there tomorrow, and frankly, I'm watching about the best floor show I've seen in ages. I'm snapping pictures like crazy to show all those know-nothings at home that they don't know Jack when they sanctimoniously tell us that St. Patrick's Day in Ireland is more of a "family" religious holiday. Yeah, right!

You think South Boston does crazy outfits? I saw more green feather boas, leprechaun top hats, green fur everything, Viking helmets with blond braids, orange braids, fright wigs, than I ever did on corn beef day at the Irish American Club. Oh, and then there was my personal favorite: the big, bare, pink, plastic fanny with the words "Kiss my Ass" – in the Irish language, of course. This is all even funnier when the wearer is about ready to kiss the floor.

So, this Monday morning, I'm not exactly at the top of my game. A plan to me would be navigating my way to the ladies' room, but my cousin says, "What're we gonna do today?" I just give him a look since going back to bed for the day is obviously not an option. "Well," he says, "do you think we should go to the parade?"

"The parade? The St. Patrick's Day Parade? Isn't that a bit too touristy? And crowded? And noisy????" My head at this point is thumping away to a tune from Riverdance. "Besides, the hairdryer in the room broke two seconds after I turned it on; I had to improvise in a hurry, and I think my hair looks weird."

"Your hair looks great."

"Really? Well, I mean, it's obviously not my hair."

"Whose hair is it?" He's asking the question like he imagines I mugged somebody in the elevator for it.

"Well, I mean, it's my hair. I bought it. It's a hair extension." I can tell he has no idea what I'm talking about, and I'm not getting into it, so I change the subject.

"OK, well, if you want to go to the parade, I need to go outside and see how cold it is because I might need a wool sweater under my raincoat if we're going to be standing out there for five hours. I'll meet you back at the room."

I slowly push away from the table and start strolling across the lobby floor. From the corner of my eye I spot a rather dapper gentleman dressed in a well-tailored navy suit, light blue shirt, maroon tie (he looks like he's running for political office in the US) who has put down his newspaper and is intently following my progress across the parquet. OK, OK, so my feminist heritage should be all insulted by this obvious staring, but I'm sixty-three years old; this is not a construction work site, and when some good-looking guy is looking intently at me, I'm smiling!

As I pass by his chair, I barely suppress a giggle, and say, "Good morning." At this, he jumps out of his chair, starts walking along side me and says, "You're an American!"

"Lucky guess," I say to him because of course as soon as any of us open our mouths over there, they know we're Americans.

"Well," he says, "is this your first trip to Ireland?"

I inform him that this is my third trip to this grand land, and assure him that, yes, I do indeed love it.

We chat back and forth; I tell him I'm going to the parade; he tells me he's not. He's on his way to County Wicklow to check in with a trainer who's working with one of his horses. He tells me his car is parked across the street, a new Camry, maroon - like his tie. He's very pleased with it. He asks me. "Will you be here tonight at the hotel?"

"No," I tell him. "We're going just outside the city to a cabaret at a dinner club called 'The Merry Plough Boys.'

"Oh, I know the place," he says. "Well, can I meet you back here at the hotel for a drink at five o'clock?"

"Well, I don't know. Are you married" I ask because there have been too many times in the past when I neglected to get the answer to that small particular.

"No, I'm divorced," he says. "What about you?"

"I'm a widow," I explain.

"Oh," he seems genuinely concerned, "I'm very sorry."

"Thank you. I can meet you for a drink, but I'm traveling with my cousin, and he'll be joining us."

"Oh, that's fine," he nods. "I'll look forward to meeting him."

Off he goes across the street. He's a little taller than I am, maybe 5'9", thick, white hair, average build, twinkly blue eyes, and the brogue! Yup, a real charmer. I'm definitely looking forward to having a drink in the bar; now I just have to break the news to my cousin that I managed to pick up a complete stranger in the lobby while I was supposed to be scouting the weather situation.

The parade is a stunning succession of wretched excesses, lasts three hours, and manages to play out in brilliant sunshine. The Irish INDEPENDENT estimates a crowd of 675,000, pretty well-behaved for the most part. We're up in Parnell Square, about half a kilometer from the Garda Station where it forms and begins. I can see the Dublin Writers' Museum diagonally across the street, probably won't have time to visit. I try to be sad about it!

At five o'clock, Gerry Carll (with two l's) is waiting for us in the pub. He tells me he's a farmer; I tell him I'm a teacher. By the end of the second pint, I know the following: he raises and sells racehorses; his farm is in County Meath (pronounce that "meet"); he has sold horses in the past year to buyers in South Africa, Saudi Arabia, and the US; the electric company is buying his and his neighbor's properties in a plan to re-grid the countryside; he is the youngest of five children; his two sisters live in England.

"How do you get a horse to South Africa?" I ask him.

"On a plane, of course."

"They travel, what, first class? Baggage?"

"No," he laughs. "They travel in a special compartment made for transporting horses. Course you have to sedate them throughout the flight to keep them calm."

"So, you stay down there in that little compartment with them?"

"No, I fly first class. I send the trainer down there with the horse."

"Oh." I'm trying not to sound too impressed. I've never managed to fly first class.

"And the Saudis buy Irish horses?"

"Oh, Jaysus, all the time. Then they pass them off as their own. Everybody knows Ireland breeds the best horses in the world!"

Modesty is definitely one of the endearing characteristics of the Irish. He finds out that we are leaving for Killarney the next morning and where we are staying.

"I'll call you at your hotel," he says. I don't believe it for a minute.

Sure enough, the next evening, the phone rings in the room. My cousin says, "It's for you. It's Gerry. He's in the lobby."

And this is how it goes for the rest of our trip. Gerry shows up around five, buys us a couple of drinks, and then whisks me off to some fabulous castle, or charming, local color eatery, making sure I see all the points of interest along the way. He asks a LOT of questions:

"Are you Catholic?"

I assure him I spent twelve years with the nuns. This would be an odd question anywhere else in the world, but here it could be a real deal-breaker.

"Could you live over here, do you think"

"Definitely, I love the country."

"Do you like horses?"

"Love 'em."

"Do you prefer the city to the country?" and so on.

The last night in Ireland, my cousin and I are staying at Cabra Castle, an almost fantasy hotel in County Cavan, which happens to be not that far from Gerry's farm in Meath. I tell him he should stay with us for dinner at the hotel, but he says there's a better castle down the road he'd like to take me to called NUALORE. The dining room overlooks a swan pond. It is another gorgeous spot, in the country, forty-FIVE shades of green. More of the same, yes, but oddly enough, I'm not bored! I'm guessing early Georgian for a time period.

"Well," he says to me over dessert, "I've been thinking about it, and I've decided I'd like to marry you."

"Would you now?" I ask, not sure if he's being funny or outrageously presumptuous.

"Yes, I would. What do you say to that?"

"I'd say no." At this point I am laughing.

He looks confused. "Why," he says, "do you not like me?"

"I like you fine. I just don't know you well enough."

"Well, you'll get to know me."

"When?"

"When you come over here for the summer. It'll be my job to convince you. I'll sweep you off your feet. Oh, we'll have a grand time. I'll take you to all the races: Kildare, Ascot, Galway. Course, you'd have to wear a fancy hat."

Hmmm, a summer in Ireland, intense flattery, the races, fancy hats. Sounds like a plan to me.

"I could do that," I tell him.

"So, you'll come?"

"Yes."

"And you'll think about marrying me?"

"I will think about it."

On the plane the next morning, my cousin tells me he thinks Gerry is a perfect gentleman. Of course from his perspective that translates into: he always picked up more than his fair share of the bar tab!

I'm not home a week when the phone rings with an international caller ID. 'Tis himself.

"I'm poppin' over to see you next week. What do you say to that?"

Well, he "pops over" about every two weeks after that, comes laden with gifts, charms my elderly aunt, and tells her she reminds him of his saintly mother. She starts hinting that I'm an ingrate for not accepting his proposal. I tell her no decisions until I come back from Ireland this summer. I'm holding out for Celtic Thunder!

We're sitting at the bar at the Charles Hotel in Cambridge on a perfect May afternoon when he tells me he's just bought a pregnant mare and since I won't let him buy me a ring, he's going to give me the foal as a gift. "Start thinking about names," he says, "and I'll send you the passport for the horse after it's born and registered. That way, it's your horse. It can't be sold without your approval." I did always fancy owning a horse, and if it's female, I like the name FIONA.

A week later he calls and says, "We need to breed the mare again a few weeks after she gives birth. I'm lining up a breeder in Kildare. Would you like to go in with me on the stud fee?"

I think, sure, why not? It is, after all, my foal that he'll be boarding, so I should kick in a bit. And, what's a stud fee? A couple of grand?

"OK. What's the stud fee?

"Fifteen thousand."

"Dollars???" I ask incredulously.

"No. Euros."

"Twenty-three thousand dollars???"

"Well, you need to have the best breeding stock."

"Gerry, darlin', there's a reason why horse racing is called the sport of kings, and that's because you need to be rich as one to indulge in it. I have no connection to royalty. No thanks."

Well, he sulks a bit, but we end on amicable terms. The next time he calls, he tells me that he's sending my ticket on Aer Lingus, and I should plan to arrive on July 6th.

"I'm lining up real estate for you to look at."

"Why do I want to look at real estate?"

"Because you'll be wantin' to know where you'll be living when you marry me."

"I haven't agreed to marry you."

"Well, of course you're going to marry me. We get along fine, and I'm crazy about you. Now, I don't know how soon you can sell your houses, but go to the bank and see what you can get in home equity, and when the properties sell, you can pay back the bank."

"Umm, what are you getting for the farm from the electric company?"

"I'm not sure yet. It's complicated."

"Umm. Ah, let me call you back on this tomorrow. It's late; I'm tired."

I'm not tired; I'm panicked. I call my cousin. He says, "OK, time to have this guy investigated."

We find a P.I. through the Irish INDEPENDENT classifieds: Liam Grady Investigations in Dublin. He agrees to do the research for $1800 Euros. Gulp! "Mr. Grady," I email, "is the price negotiable, given the relative abysmal value of the dollar to the Euro??" He agrees to a price of $1500 dollars. I send him all the information I have: photos, license plate numbers, phone numbers, and passport number (yup, I got that too!).

For the next two weeks, Mr. Grady becomes my new best friend. First news, the subject is not a property owner, at least not in his own name. The Dublin house is rented. There is no farm in Meath, no horses, no trainers. His cars are leased.

The following week: he has never been married, lied about his age, his birth date; also goes by the name of Gerard Corby. The next email says: "I have information I need to discuss with you personally. Please call the office as soon as possible."

I'm so nervous, I dial the number wrong, twice! I finally get Mr. Grady. He apologizes profusely for the character of the subject and says he hopes I won't judge all the Irish by Mr. Carll's conduct. I assure him I will not. He sounds extremely angry.

"This man," he practically hisses, "is a liar and a thief. He's a big time gambler, connected to organized crime, has several fraud charges pending against him, but here's the worst of it. Are you sitting down?" I assure him I am. "He has defrauded two women in Ireland. One, a widow in Carlow, to the tune of 200,000 euros, and another in Cork for upwards of 50,000 euros. He pretends to court them, promises marriage, and then gets them to turn over their property to him. I hope you are not terribly upset by this information?"

I tell him it's not a total surprise and that I'm fine. In fact, I'm using an Aer Lingus ticket that I have to fly over and spend a couple of weeks in Dublin. "Oh, that's lovely," he says. We chat a while longer, then I hang up and call my cousin.

"I knew it all along," he says. "The man was clearly no gentleman. Are you really flying over next week? Are you going to tell Gerry what you know?"

"I'll leave a message on his cell phone. He'll probably drive off the road when he hears it!!"

"Serve him right," my cousin comments.

"Oh, and while I'm over there, I'm going to have dinner with that nice Mr. Grady."

There is silence on the other end of the phone. Then I hear a groan.

The Bad Dates Contest

IN 2010, I ENTERED a "Bad Dates" contest. It was sponsored by the Merrimack Rep Company in Lowell, Massachusetts as a promo for their upcoming one-woman show called 300 Bad Dates. I suppose one might ask why ANYONE would want to enter a "bad dates contest." Well, I think that falls under the category of SEEMED LIKE A GOOD IDEA – AT THE TIME! Anyway, I was seduced by the prizes: two free tickets to the show, a gift certificate to La Boniche (my favorite restaurant) and a bottle of really good champagne.

It was pretty easy to come up with a winning entry because I had been doing the on-line dating thing without much success when my best friend Suzy called to tell me I'm crazy to be in cyber space, and how do I know I'm not dealing with rapists and convicts? She said I need to join a dating service where they check out the guys first, have you take a compatibility test, in other words, do some old fashioned match making.

I said, "Yeah, but some of them are pretty pricey. Like Gentle People. I heard they charge upwards of 10 grand for their service."

"OK," she said, "so that's the Cadillac of dating services, but my cousin works for one that's more the Ford Focus of match making. It's not that expensive. I'll get her discount, and did you know my cousin met her husband while working there?"

"Oh sure! They scoop up all the best guys for themselves. What kind of deal is that?"

A week later I was sitting in the office talking to Celine who assured me she has the perfect guy for me. It took about an hour to answer all the stupid questions in my compatibility profile. What kind of fish would I be if I were a fish? And would I be more upset about being overdressed than underdressed for an event? How about I wouldn't care much one way or the other?

She gave me the profile of my first match. She said to call him if he hasn't contacted me within a week. I tell her if he hasn't contacted me in a week to just send along profile #2. I can tell by the look she gave me that she was not happy with my attitude.

The first two matches were lackluster, and that's being kind. But #3 was one for the books. I suggested we meet for coffee or lunch as we'd been advised to do by our dating counselor Celine. But he insisted he wanted to take me out for dinner. We agreed to meet at seven. I arrived first, and as I'm gathering up my stuff, I noticed a battered pick-up truck, complete with gun rack, pull into the lot. Out of it steppped a Willy Nelson look alike – holding a red rose. Let's just announce over WBZ that this is a blind date! He has shoulder length white hair, cowboy boots, and a western fringed jacket complete with a string tie.

OK. Decision time. Do I cut and run, in which case what do I tell Celine? Or, do I act like an adult, take a chance, and boldly follow?

I walked into the restaurant and said, "Hi, you must be John" while looking down at someone who is six inches shorter than I am – in flats. When we're seated, he told me he lives in a trailer park where the fees are going up, and that's a real problem for people who are living on social security. Just as I'm wondering if ordering soup and salad would be an extravagance, I smell something burning. His menu is on fire. Apparently, even with his coke bottle glasses, he failed to notice the lit candle on the table. He extinguished the flames with his water glass, simultaneously drowning the bread basket. Our flustered waitress graciously escorted us to another table.

Half-way through the meal, he excused himself to use the facilities. A few seconds later, I heard a shriek. Seems like he wandered into the ladies room by mistake. As he returned to the table, I noticed there were about six inches of toilet paper stuck to his cowboy boot. I am now praying that there is no one I know in this place. We get through the meal somehow, and the check arrived. I offered to split the bill, but he insisted on picking up the tab. He left the exact amount in cash, and told me he doesn't believe in tipping. It's not up to him to subsidize the wait staff if management is too cheap to pay them a decent wage. I felt so sorry for the poor waitress that I told him I left my gloves on my chair, so I could go back and leave a ten dollar bill on the table. Out in the parking lot he said, "The night is young. How about going to a movie?"

"Oh goodness," I said sweetly, "look at the time. It's almost nine o'clock and I have a very early day tomorrow."

A month later, I'm at the Merrimack Rep early to pick up my tickets and gifts. I'm trying to be invisible, but the lady at the box office announced: "Here she is! This is the woman who won the bad dates contest!" The ushers all came running over for a look (probably had bets on how weird I was). One of the ushers said he couldn't believe I would ever have a bad date." Oh, you have no idea," I told him. "You really have No idea!"

You've Got Messages!

Welcome, Sierra Sun, to OUR TIME.com the online dating site for seniors. Great news! You have 11 matches and 7 messages today.

Message 1: Hi Sierra Sun, you deserve a flirt!
Thanks, Bay Watch Boy, you made my day!

Message 2: Sierra Sun, I'd like to get to know you. Signed, Prairie Prince, S. Dakota
Hey, Prairie Prince, S. Dakota is kind of a long way from Cape Cod. Not much of a chance of meeting for coffee.
No problem, Sierra Sun, I could come visit for a while.
Whoa, Prairie Prince, you move wa-a-y too fast for me!
Sierra Sun, you're no fun. Go to hell.
No thanks, Prairie Prince!
BLOCK SENDER

Message 3: Hi Sierra Sun, nice pictures. We should get to know each other. Ron Jon2
You could be right, Ron Jon, but you have no picture and very little info, so I don't know enough about you to make that call.
Hey, Sierra Sun, wouldn't you rather just see me in person?
OK, truth time Ron Jon. Would you be contacting me if I hadn't posted several pictures?
Waiting. Waiting. Waiting.
NO RESPONSE

Message 4: Sierra Sun, who are you kidding? Your photos don't match your age. Oldest trick in The book: bait and switch. Get real. I'm not falling for it. Signed- Canaligator

Dear Canaligator, Really, really, really glad you're not falling for it.
BLOCK SENDER

Message 5: Sierra Sun, since you did not stay in contact with me while you were on vacation, I am concluding that you do not wish to pursue this relationship. Please advise ASAP! Fairhaven Rick.

Dear Rick, I felt no need to stay in contact with anyone but my aunt Ruth, and FYI we do not HAVE a relationship!

Message 6: Hey there, Sierra Sun, you certainly look like someone I'd like to get to know. Want to chat? Fly Boy, Harwich.

Hey there, Fly Boy, real name Steve, I met you for coffee at Nirvana in Barnstable last February. Never heard from you again, so maybe getting to know me is not really a priority.

Message7: Your membership in OUR TIME will automatically renew in 10 days unless you go to "My Account" and click on "don't renew".
CLICK: MY ACCOUNT
CLICK: Don't renew
HMMMMM. I wonder if E Harmony is any good???

TRAVEL TRIUMPHS AND DISASTERS

The Rum Swizzle Inn

It was April of 1975, and Massachusetts was in the throes of celebrating the country's bicentennial. The rest of the 49 states would be honing in on the event next year in '76, but for us, 1775 was the big deal: one if by land, two if by sea; Paul Revere's ride; the march through Menotomy (Arlington); the battles of Lexington Green and Concord Bridge; re-enactments all over the place. It was definitely a good time to get out of town if possible. I thought the farthest I could hope to escape to was maybe Ogunquit, Maine.

Things began to look up considerably when I got a call from my good friend, fellow teacher, and usual sometimes partner in crime, Sharon.

"Want to go to Bermuda over April vacation?" she asked.

"Sure, if I win the lottery this weekend."

"No," she said. "It won't cost us anything but air fare. The travel company in Lexington that I started working for part-time is sending me to check out some cottages in South Hampton. We'll have a whole cottage to stay in. Plenty of room."

I'm going over in my mind the part about not costing anything but air fare. I had heard this line of reasoning from Sharon before, and inevitably things always ended up costing a lot more than the plane ticket.

"What about food, events, shopping, emergencies?" I faltered.

She glossed over that. "Yeah, but we have a place to STAY! Free!"

I guess this was supposed to offset the problem of how to finance the rest of the trip.

"We'll put the airfare on credit cards and take a couple of hundred in cash. That should be plenty." Famous last words.

Actually, I could afford to go. It was more a matter of how I wanted to spend my savings: a week at Hampton Beach in the summer with my son and friends, or a hedonistic splurge on myself in Bermuda? I told myself I had never been to Bermuda; Hampton Beach was always good for a day trip, and finally, we had a place to stay. Free!

We set about finding cheap air fare, arranging care for Sharon's mother and her dogs, and a babysitter for my son, who was eight. The babysitting part proved to be the easiest. Between two grandmothers, one doting aunt, and his father (my ex), I had the week covered. What was not so easy was my son's reaction to my departure. Floods of tears and what looked like a genuine panic attack followed my announcement.

"You can't go to Bermuda," he wailed, clutching at my shirt and hanging on for dear life. "You'll get lost in the Bermuda Triangle and never come home again." Clearly, he'd been watching too many of those "Mysteries of . . . ." shows on TV.

"Don't be silly," I said. "Bermuda is an island. The Bermuda Triangle is in a different part of the ocean, and I'll be flying from Boston which means I'll never even be near the Bermuda Triangle. Besides, nobody has disappeared into it in the last hundred years."

I was not sure this was true, but it sounded good - even to me. He still didn't look convinced, but at least he stopped bawling. I told his father to make sure he distracted him on the day we left.

We left Logan Airport on a 92 degree day, incredibly warm for the middle of April. It was 76 degrees in Bermuda! The flight was calm, and I kept looking at my watch to see if there were any magnetic fields playing havoc with it. So far, so good. Looking down on the island, I saw really pink sand and striated hues of aquamarine. The brochures told the truth. The cottages proved to be quite charming, and the next day, Sharon outlined her plans for us.

"We have to go the South Hampton Princess to get our bikes (mopeds)," she said. "They have the best ones on the island, but they make you go to bike school first before you can sign them out."

"Bike school? This is a joke, right?"

"No. They told me about it at the travel agency. Lots of people get hurt down here because they don't know the mechanics of the moped." I considered this for a moment and not being particularly mechanical myself, I began to see the wisdom of it.

Bike school was located in a big parking lot behind the South Hampton Princess hotel. It had yellow lanes painted down the length of it – lots of lanes, twenty or more. There were only six of us gathered for bike school that morning, and when the attendant wheeled over my bike, I was delighted. It was pink, island pink with a woven pink basket resting pertly on the front fender. It was hard to concentrate on what the instructor was saying. I was too eager to just escape with my wonderful new toy.

To graduate from bike school required the rider to start and stop, accelerate, ride within the lanes, brake, and park. I managed to accomplish all these tasks, although accelerating and de-accelerating caused a bit of confusion at first. Sharon, the natural adventurer, breezed through the course and got her bike before me. Her bike was blue.

"OK," she said, "now that we're mobile, we can check out the Rum Swizzle Inn up in St. George. It's the 'in' place to be on the island. It's kind of a long ride, but we can use the practice riding."

A long, beautiful ride it was down narrow lanes bordered by high green hedges, past houses that looked as if they had been transported whole from the Cotswolds. Flowering shrubs in bloom everywhere, and the air scented with Jasmine, or gardenia, or some intoxicating combination of both. Finally, as we were nearing the airport, Sharon pointed out the Rum Swizzle Inn in the distance. There were about fifty bikes parked in a row outside, and the long porch in front of the colonial-looking building was filled with patrons enjoying an afternoon cocktail.

Now was the time to practice that de-accelerating stuff and find a spot to park. OK, so was it the wrist up or down on the right handlebar? I tried up. The bike shot forward at warp speed. Before I knew it, I was doing a wheelie. The front end of the bike tipped up like a rearing stallion. "Whoa," I'm screaming as I tried to get the beast under control, "Whoa!"

I didn't get it under control, but instead plowed into the line of bikes perfectly parked out front. One by one, they fell over on their sides like a row of dominoes, brightly colored dominoes touching familiarly in the afternoon sun. I was on the ground looking up at my bike which was now covering my body like armor. I just lay there trying to assess the damage to my person.

Suddenly, it seemed like everyone who was drinking on the porch was now on the street trying to assess the damage to their machines. It took a while to untangle the mess and upright the bikes. I was wondering where Sharon was and why she wasn't offering me any assistance. Finally, I spotted her doubled over and slowly walking toward me. My first thought was, "Oh no, she's injured," but that was definitely not the case. Sharon, as the saying goes, was laughing her ass off, laughing so hard she could barely stand up. She stopped howling long enough to pull the bike off me, lend me her hand and help me up. I could stand, move, nothing broken, no blood, probably a few bruises would appear in the morning, but I was lucky. God does indeed take care of children and fools.

We walked up the steps to the inn, and at a table near the door was a middle-aged man in golf clothes, bent over like Sharon was, and again, a la Sharon, he was laughing his ass off. Before we could pass by his table, he straightened up, grabbed my hand, still laughing, and asked, "Where are you two girls from?" We said Boston, that being the most recognizable city to our actual residence.

"Well, Boston ladies, I haven't laughed that hard in years. The best part was you yelling 'Whoa' as you wiped out the whole parking lot." Now, he's laughing again, but still has my hand in his grip. "I'm taking you inside to meet the bartender because you two are drinking free on my tab for the rest of the day." He then doubled over again, tears coming to his eyes. "Damn, I haven't laughed that hard in years!"

And, drink away the afternoon on his tab we did. We tried every intriguing concoction in the bar. When it was finally time to call it quits, Sharon said, "Wow, we really drank a lot. Ya think we can drive?"

"Course we can drive," I assured her, "cause we sure as hell can't walk!"

The state we were in, this made perfect sense to us, and we mounted up for the long ride back to our cottage. I sort of remember some of the scenery. At one point, I bounced off a wall, but got right back on the bike again – as one should always do after wiping out! I know we made it back to the cottage because that's where I woke up the next morning.

I loved my week in Bermuda. We explored, shopped, swam, but nothing else quite equaled the adventure of the Rum Swizzle Inn. At the airport, waiting to go home, I surveyed my fellow travelers. Some had arms in casts, some had legs in casts, some were bandaged, bruised, some in neck braces. I said to Sharon, "Bike accidents. Wow, you know, it's a good thing we went to that bike school. That could be us."

She gave me a look, and then we both totally cracked up!

The Road's Washed Out

IN THE SUMMER OF 2008, I decided to spend a few weeks in Dublin, Ireland. I happened to have in my possession a free round trip airline ticket, and how that came to be is a story for another day. Suffice to say that on all my other trips to that enchanting isle, I had been confined to one or two days in the city, and had left always wishing there had been time to see more. This was my chance to satisfy a longing that had been gnawing at my curiosity for years.

In late July, I went on-line to find a hotel that would be affordable and convenient for a few weeks in August. It was peak tourist season, but not having yet retired, I had limited choices. Everything in the city was either already booked or prohibitively expensive. Finally, I chanced upon the Port Marnock Hotel, a golf and conference center about seven miles north of the city. It had been the summer home of the Jameson family, famous for Jameson Irish whiskey, and the main building was a stately, old Victorian mansion right on the ocean. It looked lovely in the pictures: I guess you can't go wrong selling whiskey to the Irish! Now it boasted an 18 hole golf course, several newer buildings, and a pub located in the former library of the house. I contacted the desk and found out I had my choice of a "garden" view room or an ocean view.

"What's the difference?" I asked.

"About $160 a night," I was told.

I decided that I really was very fond of gardens, and that I didn't need to pay extra for an ocean view. I was getting a good rate anyway since I was staying for three weeks, and the extra money would go towards shopping and the theater. So, I booked the room and started packing.

Now, I had traveled on my own to several closer destinations: Williamsburg, Virginia; the Canadian Maritimes; Burlington, Vermont; Bar Harbor. But, this would be my first European adventure solo. I was a little apprehensive, but I overcame my doubts with the facts that first, I had been there before, and second, it was an English speaking country, and I did, after all, have a tongue in my mouth. As usual, on the overnight flight from Logan, I couldn't get much sleep. I had my neck pillow, my eye shade, and soothing music in my ear phones, but still only managed about half an hour! So, when I landed at Dublin airport at 5:00 a.m. on a Sunday morning I was red-eyed and nerve wracked.

My plan was to collect my luggage and find a taxi to take me the five or six miles to Port Marnock. I had paid the hotel for the previous night so that when I arrived early on Sunday morning, my room would be ready and I could check in right away. They would be expecting me. Departing through the front doors of the terminal, I looked over to where the usual line of cabs should be parked. There was not a cab in sight. Hmmm. That's odd. Then, I thought, well, it's Sunday morning. They're just not here yet. It occurred to me to ask at the information kiosk about the cab situation, but it was shuttered tight. Nothing appeared to be open or functioning except a coffee machine. I had some coins left from my last visit, got a watery cup, and sat down with my book to await the awakening of the terminal.

About three hours later, the information kiosk raised up its shutters, and I strolled over to find out about the taxi cab situation.

"Well, there are no taxis this morning. They're all stuck in Dublin. Haven't you heard? There was a terrible rain storm last night and the roads are washed out."

"But I need to get to Port Marnock," I explained.

"Oh, that's no problem," he said. "You can get the bus. It's the number 110 bus, and it goes right through Port Marnock."

"Where can I get it?" I asked.

"Well," he said, "you walk all the way through this terminal, cross the street, go into the next terminal and walk through that, and you'll come out to the car park. You'll see a little sign that shows where the bus stops and you wait there."

"OK. Sounds good. What time is the next bus?"

He checked his schedule and declared, "ten thirty."

The Road's Washed Out

Ah, still two hours to wait. Back to my bench and my book which was rapidly approaching its concluding chapter. I was getting hungry about now, but none of the other concessions at the terminal had opened yet.

At ten o'clock, I gathered up my huge suitcase, my carry-on, my purse, and my coat and headed out to the bus stop. It was an arduous walk through the two terminals weighted down as I was, but I spotted the bus stop sign and sat down on my suitcase to wait. I had not slept for 30 hours now, and was feeling jittery exhausted. After an hour had passed, I concluded that there was no bus coming, so I collected my baggage and trekked back to terminal one and my buddy at the information kiosk. I reported that I had waited at the bus stop for an hour, but no number 110 bus had come by.

"Well," he explained, "you can't expect the buses to be running on schedule today, not after last night. You know the roads are washed out."

At this point, I was contemplating buying a ticket on the next flight home. Then, I began to get stern with myself. "You are not the type of woman who folds under a little bit of adversity. Buck up. You will figure this out!"

So, back I trudged through the two terminals out to the car park to sit again and await the number 110 bus. Breakfast was a granola bar I managed to score from a vending machine after begging some change from a stewardess, but I couldn't bear the thought of another cup of watery coffee. Finally, at eleven forty-five, wonder of wonders, the number 110 bus arrived. I asked the driver if this is indeed the bus that goes to Port Marnock, and he assured me it was. I felt like I'd just won the lottery as he loaded my luggage into the back of the bus. About a mile down the road, I saw what appeared to be a very large puddle covering the road. Next, the bus was swerving and curving, then finally floated over to the side in a kind of gully. We were leaning at about a forty-five degree angle inside and trying to steady ourselves from sliding onto the floor.

The bus driver, visibly shaken, told everyone to stay put. He opened the door and stepped into waist deep water. I could see him calling on his cell phone before he opened the back door of the bus, unloaded my luggage, then helped each of us up the side of a hill which was conveniently located on the opposite side of the road. I was now wet up to my knees, even more exhausted, and sitting on my suitcase awaiting further instructions. Flashing lights signaled the arrival of the Garda who blocked off both sides of the road with saw horse barriers. The bus driver assured us that we would all be taken to our destinations as soon as help arrived.

Help arrived about fifteen minutes later in the person of Thomas Flaherty, driving a very large, new, black Mercedes.

"Hello," he greeted us. "I'm Thomas Flaherty, the president of the Dublin Bus Company, and I'm here to see that you all get delivered to your doorstops." There were four of us at this point, and Mr. Flaherty found out that two were bound for the town of Swords, one for Malahide, and I was going to Port Marnock.

"Where in Port Marnock?" he asked. I gave him the address, and he said, "Oh, you're staying at the country club. That's what we call it. Lovely place."

That was the first cheerful news I had heard all morning. Sure enough, each of my fellow passengers was dropped off at his home, and I was the last, sitting in the back seat of this impressive vehicle, when we pulled into the long driveway of the Port Marnock Hotel and Conference Center. Mr. Flaherty pulled up to the entrance, got out of the car, unloaded my luggage from the trunk, then helped me out of the back seat. The bell hops were tripping over each other to see who would grab my luggage, the front desk clerk was standing in the doorway, and a few guests were gawking out the window. Let me say, it was quite an arrival. I thanked Mr. Flaherty profusely for his rescue, and proceeded up the steps to the lobby.

"Hello," I said to the desk clerk. "I'm Mrs. Barrett, and I have a reservation."

"Oh, Mrs. Barrett," she said, "we expected you early this morning."

"Well," I said, "maybe you haven't heard, but the roads are washed out."

"Oh, it was a terrible storm last night." She was shuffling papers around, and making changes on the computer monitor. I thought, "Hmm, maybe my room isn't ready after all."

"I see we've assigned you a garden view room, but I think you'd be much happier with an upgrade," she assured me.

"Thank you, I'm sure I would," I told her.

I followed the bell hop up to the third floor of the old mansion. He opened the door to a lovely, corner-room suite complete with ocean and golf course view, a dressing room, a bath with a Jacuzzi tub, a tea table in front of a bow window, and a small, but charming living room. I loved it, and it would be my home for the next three weeks. I can only say that I had Mr. Flaherty and his fancy Mercedes to thank for my good fortune, and of course, the crazy weather.

I tipped the bell hop and asked him about a little Italian restaurant that had been recommended to me in Malahide.

"Oh, I wouldn't be goin' up there this afternoon, Mrs. Barrett. Haven't you heard? The road's washed out."

Not So Fine Dining

I HAVE RECENTLY RETURNED FROM a wonderful ten-day trip to Madeira Island and San Miguel Island in the Azores. Madeira is not in the Azores, but is in an archipelago, a two-hour flight south of the Azores. It's off the coast of Africa and much closer to the equator; hence, warmer and more populated by European tourists escaping dreary climates. Both islands had spectacular scenery, quaint little villages, friendly natives, and a leisurely pace of life. As stunning as all this was, what I will always remember most about that vacation was dinner at Ixtapa on our first night in Porta Delgada, San Miguel. Our tour guide, Sue, had touted the fact that this was a new place, very trendy, and famous for its amazing seafood. I was traveling with a group of seventeen people, all from Cape Cod, and all quite familiar after a week of adventures in the mountains of Madeira. She said the restaurant had a transport service that would pick us up at the hotel at 6:30 that evening. So, at 6:25, we were all standing in little groups around the lobby waiting.

At 6:45, as we were getting fidgety, Sue announced that the restaurant had called and there would be a delay until 7:00 p.m. Now these are Americans, more used to eating dinner at six or before, as opposed to the European model of starting to order appetizers at 8:30. The hotel manager heard us grumbling and came out with two big pitchers of iced tea and real little glasses – no plastic, thank you very much. Finally, at 7:15, two vans pulled up, and we all piled in. The restaurant, which was a bit out of the way in the suburbs, was very modern and sleek with floor to ceiling windows on all sides, and a huge aquarium in the center of the room which might be holding our dinners. I hoped the food would make up for Ixtapa's lack of old-world charm which was sadly missing. We were seated at a very long banquet table in the center of the place – eight couples on each side and me, solo, at the head of the table. This made me a bit apprehensive as I imagined I could be mistaken for the responsible party paying the bill. The other odd thing about this was that we were practically the only people in the place on a Sunday evening. Well, the first order of business was getting a drink. There appeared to be only one waiter in the place, and he was taking care of a few tables at the far end. After twenty minutes went by, Sue went in search of someone to complain to.

Soon after, our waiter appeared. Interestingly enough, he was also our van driver! We explained that we wanted 9 separate checks: one for each couple and one for me. He agreed that it was no problem and took our drink orders. The drinks started being delivered one at a time, at intervals of several minutes. The reason for this: our waiter was also the bartender and making the drinks himself. People started sharing their drinks with those still waiting. I never did get mine, but Marianne ended up with two and gave me hers. At this point we're getting silly. Fred said, "Hey, Sue. We really love this restaurant. Could you go ask them if they serve food?"

It was now nine o'clock, and the restaurant began filling up with people. I noticed there were lots of families, and I wondered about keeping the kids out that late. Two more waiters appeared to deal with the influx. We still had the van driver. We insisted that we get some bread, and he brought a couple of baskets for the whole table. I thought Jim and Fred were going to go head to head over the last piece. Our waiter took appetizer orders along with entrees to save time, I guess. Another fifteen minutes passed and the appetizers started to arrive. For those who had not ordered appetizers, there was still no food. We noticed another oddity. Our waiter/van driver was going into the kitchen for prolonged periods of time. Could it be he was making the appetizers??

It took another half hour for the entrees to appear. Why? Our server waited until those who ordered appetizers had finished. Just about everyone ordered fish, and when it began to arrive, there was a common complaint. It was incredibly overcooked. Each plate looked as if it had sat in the warming oven for the past two days. Some of the species were unrecognizable. Fred sent his back saying he ordered grilled swordfish, not cremated swordfish. It was impossible to get tartar sauce or any mitigating condiments to moisten the arid filets on our plates. We made do with the sides, which were tasty if not readily recognizable.

If you think people were angry, guess again. For one thing, we were all on vacation, and for another, when things go this terribly wrong it starts to get funny. Each new gaffe or outrage brought out the jokes and witty comments. We were just getting plain silly and laughing at everything. At eleven o'clock, the word went up and down the table: "If anyone orders dessert, he will be left behind and made to walk back to the hotel!" We were afraid dessert might be served with our morning coffee.

Our waiter/van driver handed the bill to Sue. Separate checks? Not a chance. He suggested we just split it 17 ways. Well, that almost caused a mutiny. The no alcohol vegetarians were not about to bail out the two-drink, three appetizer gourmands. So, we told him we would go to the cashier, one at a time, and settle each individual meal. He would just have to take our word for what we ordered. But look! The cashier is (wait for it!) also our waiter/van driver/bartender/ sous chef. It only took another thirty minutes to settle up and get back in the vans for the ride back.

I woke up my roommate as I stumbled into the bathroom after midnight. She had chosen to go with a friend to a little bistro down near the waterfront. "How was everything at Ixtapa?" she asked. I told her that she missed a really fun time and that I was sore from laughing!

How To Get Along in France

It was along ride from Brugge, Belgium to Paris, and after regaling us for a couple of hours with tales of local history, our tour guide, Adarom, switched to a catalog of French manners and customs. This was in part, I think because he did not want us to embarrass him as we trotted behind him all over the city, and partly because he had honed this routine into a fairly amusing take on cultural differences.

"You Americans have a saying, I believe, that goes something like 'the customer is always right,' no?"

"That's right," we all chimed in.

"Well, the first thing you have to understand about France is that the customer is always wrong. The second thing is that we are set in our ways. If we stop serving lunch at 3:00 p.m., and you come in at 2:30, you will not be seated. Why? Because, we want to leave at three o'clock. You might say, 'But we have a party of four, and we will spend a lot of money in your restaurant.' You will then be told to try the restaurant down the street. We don't accommodate or change our routine, and certainly not for money."

"So," we asked, "it's not personal, right?"

"Exactement. It is not personal. It is just the way we do business. Another thing that is not personal is this. We will not smile at you; we will not ask you how you are; we will not introduce ourselves. Also, we are not in a hurry. You can sit at a table for hours if you wish. You won't be presented with a bill unless you ask for it, and when you ask for it, we are not in a hurry either."

Then, Adoram launched into an anecdotal story of culture shock on his first visit to America. He was with his sister, and they went to a small restaurant in Florida. "Well," he said, "we walked in and a woman handed us menus. With a big smile she said, 'Hi, y'all. My name is Sandy, and

I'll be taking care of you today.' After seating us, she asked, 'So, how are you two doing today? Just visiting, or y'all new to town?'

"My sister whispered to me, 'Do you know her??' I shook my head, but I was thinking it's none of her business how I'm doing or why I'm here. Then, a young man wandered over with a pitcher of water and a big smile. 'Hi, my name is Greg. Can I pour you some water? It sure is warm out there. So where are y'all from?' He then proceeded to recite all the specials for the day. Sandy came by a couple of times to make sure Greg was taking good care of us, and did we need anything we didn't already have. My sister and I just wanted to be left alone! This is the kind of attention you will never get in France, and it may be your culture shock, but now you have been warned."

"The next thing you need to know is the meaning of 'bonjour.' The French always greet each other with 'bonjour.' This is not simply another form of hello. This precedes every social interaction because it is an acknowledgment of the other's personhood, humanity. So even if you speak no French, you will start your question or comment with 'bonjour' and wait for a 'bonjour' in reply. If you skip this form of politeness, you will be ignored."

"The French," he continued, "especially in shops, do not multi-task. If a clerk is waiting on a customer and appears to be almost finished, do not assume that you can ask a question. It is not your turn, and you will be waved aside or totally ignored. You may be in a hurry, but he or she is not! The French do not make change. If you go to a patisserie, order a croissant, and hand the clerk a 20 euro bill, you will be scowled at or worse! Always be polite. Learn these phrases: *excusez moi, s'il vous plait*, and *merci*. Never, under any circumstances should you snap your fingers for attention. The opposite will happen. You will cease to exist. Never, but never, refer to a waiter as 'garcon.' It means boy. If you can't manage 'Monsieur' then 'Sir' will do."

"Don't expect everyone to speak English. You are in a foreign country and the official language is French. Usually, in any establishment SOMEONE will speak English and will come to your assistance, so just be patient. If you want to blend in in Paris, wear black. If you want to look like an American tourist, wear jeans, sneakers, and a sweatshirt with your hometown logo. And finally, let's put to rest the notion that the French don't like Americans. Of course, we like Americans. We are very mindful of the fact that you saved our ass in two world wars! Not to mention the fact that Americans have a reputation for generosity and tip even when it's not necessary! Accept cultural differences; keep an open mind, and enjoy Paris."

And that, my friends, is how to get along in France!

The Moon, the Stars, and Keys

I'M REALLY NOT ONE to live my life by alignment of the stars, the trajectory of the moon, or other superstitions, but occasionally a series of occurrences will make me pause to reconsider. One such occasion happened on my last visit to Florida. I go down to Coconut Creek, near Pompano and Ft. Lauderdale, for a few weeks every winter to get out of the New England winter and visit with my old friends from when I spent the entire winter there, as the quintessential "snow bird."

On day two of my vacation, as I was preparing to head out in my rental car, I could not find the car key (or fob as its now known). I ALWAYS put it in the front zipper compartment of my purse. Well, maybe NOT always because it's not there. I search every surface of the condo, look under the bed, the couch, empty wastebaskets, check every pocket of clothing I've worn – nothing! Now what? Do I call Avis and tell them I've lost a key and can they bring me another one? Will they actually do that? Or, do I have to somehow get myself back to the airport to pick up another one? How ditsy will I look if I do this? Maybe I could tell them the key was stolen, but, who steals a key and not the car with it? That's it! The car has been stolen. I run to the window to verify that fact; alas, there is indeed a silver GMC Terrain parked in spot #153. Wait! There is one final, if unlikely explanation. I left the key in the car. Ridiculous. I would never do anything so stupid and irresponsible. I head down to the parking lot to reassure myself that that scenario is just wrong. The door handle opens effortlessly. OK, so I didn't lock it. I get in and voila! There in the cup holder is the key fob. I am banging my head on the steering wheel in relief and chagrin.

Day number three of my Florida vacation. I have done my mile and a half walk around the complex circle; I'm a little warm, so I decide to head to the pool. I know I will probably be the only person there because it is ten o'clock in the morning; the temperature is 75 degrees, and the natives would consider that WAY too chilly to go swimming. I was correct. After forty-five blissful minutes of swimming leisurely laps, I drip my way back to the condo. Reaching into my beach bag, I feel my phone, towel, book, sun screen, glasses, hat, but not my key to the place. This key is hard to miss. It is on a spiral stretchy bracelet in hot pink with a plastic flamingo dangling from it. Now what? Fortunately, I do have my phone. I can call security to let me in. What I don't have is the number for security. I call my friend, Sharon, who lives in another building. "I can't call security for you," she says. "it's against the rules." Ah, yes, the endless bureaucracy of the condo KGB!

"OK," I tell her. "Just give me the number and I'll call." She starts rattling off the digits. "Wait, wait! I'm in a bathing suit with a beach bag. I don't have anything to write with. Just text me the number." I get security on the line and they tell me they'll be there in five minutes. In less than that, I am conversing with Lt. Kelley who asks me if I am the owner. I tell him no, I'm just visiting. He tells me he can't let me in because I am not the owner and I have no identification. "My identification is in the condo, in my purse, and furthermore I am registered with security so I can get in and out of the complex, and if you call, they can verify that." He says that's not good enough and can I call the owner. I tell him I can, but she's at work and I don't like to disturb her. He tells me I have to. OK. I get Trudi on the line. She vouches for the fact that I am staying in her condo and that he should open the door for me. He says he will if she can give him her security code pin number. "It's on my desk in the den," she says, "and I don't remember what it is because I never have to use it."

"Well," he says to me, "that's it. I can't let you in."

"Seriously? Are you telling me that you are going to let me stand here in a wet bathing suit all day?"

"You can go get the key from where your friend works."

"I am in a wet bathing suit, and the car key is in the house."

"You can call a cab."

"You want me to wander through the Promenade Mall in a wet bathing suit and flip flops with no money to pay the cab driver because my purse is in the house? Look, you know my friend Trudi. She's lived here for eleven years. You talked to her on the phone. There is no reason you can't let me in!"

"It's against the rules, but I'll make an exception." He is opening the door now. "You know I'm not supposed to be doing this."

"Thanks, but please come in." My purse is on the dining room table. I give him a ten-dollar tip and thank him for his time. Just one more reason I'm glad I don't live here anymore!

The next day my friend and former neighbor, Bob, calls to ask if I would like to go out for dinner that night. I say "Sure," and he says he'll make a reservation at the Capitol Grille in Boca. Nice. I've never been to that one.

It's a beautiful night, full moon, 75 degrees. Because it's Boca, the restaurant is even swankier than usual. It looks like an English gentleman's private club. Not that I've ever been in such a place, but I do watch a lot of BBC programs on PBS. We have a lovely, leisurely dinner and about nine-thirty ask the valet to bring the car around. Bob has a white Lexus sedan with a black leather interior which he bought last year. The valet hands him the key; we get in and head down the Florida Turnpike towards Coconut Creek. About ten minutes into the drive, Bob has a puzzled look on his face. "June," he says, "I don't think this is my car."

"Of course, it's your car," I tell him. "Why do you think that?"

"The console looks different," he says.

"Well that's because we had the radio on, and now it's on GPS. You know those guys always fool around with things when they take the car."

"No. It's different." He tells me to look in the glove compartment. I open it and come up with an application for a Sun Pass.

"Is this yours?" I ask.

"No!" he says. Just then his phone rings.

"Bob, why is your phone ringing? You have Blue Tooth." He pulls over to the side of the Turnpike and answers it. I can hear the conversation.

"Hello, is this Dr. Woodruff?"

"Yes, it is."

"Dr. Woodruff, I'm afraid there's been a mistake made by the valet team. It seems the car you're driving belongs to another diner, and your car is here in front of the restaurant. How far away are you?"

"We can be there in about fifteen minutes."

We get off at the next exit and get back on the highway heading north. We go through a couple of toll booths, and Bob says, "I hope that guy did get a Sun Pass. If not, he's going to get billed for these tolls."

"Oh my God, do you realize we are driving a stolen car? This is too funny! I haven't been in a stolen car since high school!"

By this time, we are both laughing hysterically, and playing the "What if" game. "What if we get in an accident? Whose insurance pays for it? What if we get stopped by the State Police for speeding (which we were)?"

We get back to the restaurant to find the valet team looking white-faced and stricken. They are tripping over each other trying to explain what happened. Apparently both cars were called for at exactly the same time looking exactly alike, and we, being out front first got into the car to which they had opened the doors! The other gentleman, who has been waiting half an hour for the return of his car, is clearly not amused. I walk over and start talking to his wife. She's very nice, and we both think the whole thing is a hoot. After all, it is, as I've mentioned, a beautiful night. Bob is having a heated conversation with her husband.

When we finally get into the right car and are headed back to Coconut Creek, Bob tells me the other guy was pissed and decided it was Bob's fault for not realizing the mistake right away. "Maybe I should have checked the license plate before we got in," he muses.

"Don't be silly. Nobody does that. We've done valet parking many times before and never checked the license plate number! Besides, this was an adventure. We'll be laughing about this for years!"

Now Bob is not one to accept paranormal explanations for things, but I am firmly convinced that this third event in my vacation featuring a key was no coincidence. A full moon? The stars? An encroaching pandemic? Things are definitely out of alignment. Oh, and by the way, I'm flying home on Friday the thirteenth!

June Bowser-Barrett

FRIENDS

(WHO MOSTLY TALKED ME INTO THIS CRAZY STUFF)

The Housewarming Gift

Now, before I start this story, I need to make it very clear that I love dogs. Growing up, I always had a dog. My first word was not "Mama" or "DaDa" but "Woody," the name of the family dog. So, imagine my surprise when I came to realize that there was actually a dog I didn't like. No, that's too mild a term for my loathing of this particular pooch and breed.

He belonged to my good friends Jack and Meg who lived in Brewster, and who were my very generous hosts on many a Cape getaway. His name was Caesar and he was a medium Schnauzer. I think they were bred to be rat terriers, and the rat part was certainly true. This dog was out of control. A ringing doorbell would send him into a frenzy of barking that lasted a good five minutes accompanied by lunging at the guest, and the baring of teeth. My hosts, Jack and Meg, did not seem bothered at all by this behavior, maybe thinking he was a good watchdog. It was impossible to carry on a conversation while this demonstration of protectiveness went on. He liked to get your attention by scratching on your leg whether you were wearing jeans or shorts, and that was sometimes followed by a very vigorous humping of said leg, to the huge amusement of his pet parents. He barked at every little noise day and night, so that it was not possible to sleep soundly through any night. My hosts were pretty much insomniacs anyway, so they took no steps to control this behavior in Caesar. I had visions of controlling the behavior with a gun!

I have not had the pleasure of owning a dog in my adult years. Living in apartments in the city was not conducive to canine cohabitation. I switched over to owning cats who were quiet and with some cunning could be hidden from landlords and nosy neighbors. When I finally bought a house with a fenced in yard and some good acreage, my friends Jack and Meg were delighted for me. They were of course on hand for the housewarming party and couldn't wait to present me with their housewarming gift which was waiting in the van. Peering in the tinted van window, I could make out what looked like a pet carrier. This was odd, I thought. The van door slid open and Jack triumphantly presented me with my gift – a Schnauzer puppy. "Oh," he effused, "we have been waiting for years to get a dog for you, and now that you have the perfect house for it, we bought you the perfect dog, a little Schnauzer! I know you'll love him as much as we love Caesar!"

To say I was speechless is an understatement. Not only was I not ready for a dog - any dog - and certainly not a Schnauzer, but I had a cat, a big malevolent Tom cat who hated everything on this earth except for me. His disgust for dogs was palpable. "Oh," I stammered. "I don't know what to say. This is just too generous, and you shouldn't have. I really can't accept this. It's just too much."

"Not at all," said Meg, hugging me. "You're one of our oldest friends and we wanted to do something special for you!"

Well, the pooch was loosed in the back yard for the duration of the party, and except for watering every bush in the yard and many chair legs, he was kind of cute. The real horror started after the guests were gone. The cat climbed down from the tree he was ensconced in and made for the dog who proceeded to bark and chase him around the yard until the cat unleashed the full fury of his claws into the pup's snout. This set up a howl that could set teeth on edge. What ensued was a week of open warfare.

My friend Linda called to see how things were going a week into the great Schnauzer intrusion experiment. "OMG, Linda, my house is chaotic. I can't live like this!"

"What are you going to do?" she asked.

"I don't know. I just know I can't keep him. I haven't even named him yet. I can't bring myself to believe he's a permanent fixture."

"Maybe you could drop him off at the shelter?" Linda is definitely not an animal lover.

"No, I can't do that. What if nobody adopts him? There's no Lucky Dog Ranch here. Brandon McMillan is not going to rush in with his red training collar and find him his forever home."

"What if he finds his own home? I mean just leave the gate to the yard open and see if he finds his own new owners."

"You know, that's an idea. He is cute and that may go a long way to some family wanting to adopt him."

The next day, after letting him out for his morning run, I did leave the gate open. Sure enough, he made his escape. I kept checking the yard throughout the day to see if he was still absent. By 7:00 p.m. it looked like he was a goner. The cat, for the first time in a week, was being affectionate again and acting like things were back to normal. I went to bed feeling a little guilty but luxuriating in a once more peaceful house.

I awoke the next morning to barking and scratching at the front door. Himself was wanting his breakfast and made a beeline for the kitchen and his feeding bowl. I kept him confined to the kitchen with a baby gate when I wasn't home, but in the interest of convenience it stayed open when I was. One night after a lengthy phone conversation with my aunt, I went looking for him. I found him in the hall closet, happily chewing on my leather boots. This was after he chewed what he could reach of my leather coat, which subsequently transitioned into my leather jacket!

Another phone call to Linda. "I am losing it," I told her. "Now, he's chewing everything in sight. I leave him out in the yard all day so he won't poop in the house, but the neighbors are complaining about his barking. I'm at my wits end."

"You have to tell Meg and Jack that he's sick."

"What? Why? He's not sick."

"I know, but here's the strategy. It worked for my sister-in-law. She was taking care of her friend's cat while her friend was in Europe for a month. The first week, the cat keeled over and died. Heart attack, stroke? Who knows? Anyway, she emailed her friend that the cat looked sick and she was taking it to the vet's. The next week, the cat was at the cat hospital for treatment. The following week, the vet was worried and couldn't diagnose the problem. The third week, the cat was gravely ill. Before the owner got home, my sister-in-law emailed her with the tragic news. My sister-in-law was thanked for her diligence and concern, and she didn't lose a friend. Now, that's what you need to do."

"Well, didn't her friend want to know how the cat was disposed of?"

"Yeah, of course she buried the cat, I mean it died a month earlier after all, but she gave her friend a box of ashes supposedly from the pet crematory."

"There's a pet crematory?"

"Definitely. But I think the ashes came from the firepit in her backyard."

"Oh my God!" I was reminded of the old adage: "Desperate times demand desperate measures."

The next day I emailed Meg that I was taking the dog to the vet's because he was having stomach issues. One week later, he was no better, and the vet was flummoxed. I then put an ad in the local paper, extolling the virtues of this puppy and that I was devastated at having to give him up due to severe allergies. By the third week, I was preparing Meg and Jack for the worst, and they were, unfortunately blaming themselves and the breeder. I got a couple of queries about adopting the dog. One from an older woman who wanted a companion, hmmm, not a good fit, and one from a grandmother who wanted a dog for her three very active grandchildren. That's better, I decided, and set up a meeting time with her. I was definitely getting tired of letting the pooch out every hour and having my kitchen smell like puppy pads every morning.

A few days before I was to meet the prospective new dog owner, I got a call from Meg, who was in tears. "We have some very sad news. Caesar has been diagnosed with cancer. It's very advanced and there's nothing they can do for him except keep him comfortable. I can't imagine life without him. Jack is walking around in a fog. We're trying to decide whether or not to put him down. I mean would it be better to let him go now or prolong his suffering because we can't part with him?"

"I think you just answered that question. You've always done what's best for Caesar. It's about his welfare, not yours. I am so sorry this happened. You must be in shock."

My next communique from Meg was that Caesar had left this earth at 9:45 a.m. on Tuesday. There were all kinds of angels and angel wings, and an RIP "All Dogs Go to Heaven" banner at the bottom. I was unkindly thinking that Caesar just may be the exception to that sentiment. I went to CVS to get a sympathy for the loss of your pet card. Then I called the grandmother to cancel our appointment.

I was up early the next morning preparing for the drive to Brewster. I packed the car with dog toys, baby gate, dog food, doggie treats, and of course the nameless pooch in a pet carrier in the back seat. "We are going to your new forever home," I told him as I backed out of the driveway.

I pulled into their driveway just under the sign that said Zephyr's Crest, the name of their property. I didn't want to take a chance at rejection by having the dog still in the car, so I scooped him up in my arms and knocked on the back door. Jack answered looking alarmed. "Oh, no, is he still really sick?"

"It's a miracle," I announced. "All this time it was a food allergy. So, the vet changed his dog food and he's been just perfect ever since. But, I'm here because I feel your pain so keenly about losing Caesar, and I think it's only fair that you have this dog to cheer you up and love. I've only had him for about a month, so it won't be gut-wrenching for me, and you are such perfect pet parents. I couldn't begin to give him the life that you will." With that, I handed over the dog to Jack. Meg heard this whole conversation and burst into tears.

"That is the most generous, selfless thing I've ever witnessed," she sobbed, hugging me. "You are truly a great friend,"

It was difficult for me to contradict that accolade, so I didn't. However, there were a couple of other old adages running through my mind. "All's well that ends well," and "What you don't know can't hurt you."

The House Guest From Hell

I USED TO SPEND WINTERS in Florida. I loved the place from December through April, but after that, I found the heat intolerable. I also loved my condo and most of my neighbors, but going back and forth from Massachusetts to Florida every year got old pretty fast. I finally sold the place in 2015. In April of 2016, my neighbor, Shirley, from my old building in Coconut Creek, called to say she was coming to New England in June, with her two sisters, to attend the graduation of their great nephew in Maine. Could they stop off in Sandwich for a night on their way north?

I thought this was a great idea because I know her sisters and have always liked them; I have room to put them up, and it would be a fun reunion. In June, Shirley called to say that she would be arriving on her way back from Maine, but her sisters would not be staying because they were running late. They would be dropping her off somewhere on I95 and could I meet them at a rest stop?

I waited for four hours at the I95 rest stop at exit 13 in Canton. They couldn't seem to find it. And there was a good reason for that: they were on 495 south! I asked where they were on 495, and they didn't know. GPS? Nope. Too newfangled. They're following Uncle Joe's directions scribbled on a napkin. I told them to get off at the next exit, go to a MacDonald's or something, tell me what exit, and I will meet them there. I finally caught up with them in Easton. While we were loading Shirley's suitcases into the back of my car, Judy shook my hand and said, "You are an absolute saint to be doing this!" The inspiration for these words became clearer as Shirley's visit unfolded.

It took several hours to get back to Sandwich in afternoon traffic. During this ride I discovered that Shirley was not spending a night or two, but that she had a flight back to Ft. Lauderdale in a week. The following day she spent in bed, exhausted from her "ordeal" of the previous day. She complained about the cold constantly. It was only in the high 60's! She couldn't figure out how to work the TV remote in her room, and constantly called me in to change channels. The following day she stayed in bed until noon, and told me it was OK for me to have lunch ready when she got out of the shower.

That evening we were invited to a dinner party at my cousin's in Mashpee. I told Shirley she would really like the house on the lake and that we would be going out in the boat for drinks and appetizers. "I can't go out in a boat," she said.

"Why can't you go out in a boat?"

"Well, you know I get seasick."

"You can't get seasick on a lake! That's why it's called Seasickness. You get sick on the SEA."

"Well, I might. I don't want to take a chance!"

"Fine. You can sit up on the deck while we're cruising around."

"No, I can't. I'll be too cold. Do you have a warm jacket I can borrow? It's freezing!"

On Sunday, there was a big family party at my cousin Pam's in Pelham, NH. I told Shirley this was a great opportunity to see more of New England.

"I can't go," she said indignantly.

"Why not"

"Well, I'm exhausted from yesterday. We didn't get home until ten o'clock from your cousin's and I missed my nap yesterday."

Actually, this was the best news I'd had in several days. After making her sandwiches for lunch, I escaped to the north. When I returned at eight o'clock, Shirley was starving.

"I ate those sandwiches at noon, and I haven't had anything to eat since! I want to go out for dinner. Where's there good barbecue around here?"

She arose the next day at noon, feeling terrible. Probably had something to do with the ribs, fries, and chili she ate the night before. "I have to go to the emergency room," she announced.

"Shirley," I explained, "that could mean three or four hours of waiting around to be seen. Are you sure it isn't indigestion?"

"I could be having a heart attack," she whined.

Four hours later, she emerged from Stoneman Clinic with a smile on her face and a spring in her step. "Oh, I feel so much better. I just needed to be told that there's nothing wrong with me!"

That evening, she asked me if I knew there was a lot of dust under the vanity in the guest bathroom. I declined to reply. Then she said, "I've been here four days already, and I haven't seen much of Cape Cod!"

"Well, Shirley," I seethed, "if you spend two days in bed and one day in the emergency room, and another afternoon in the nail salon, it kind of cuts into your sightseeing time."

"Well, I think we should go to Provincetown tomorrow."

On the way to Provincetown, we stopped every half hour so Shirley could find a bathroom. We could only drive through P Town because all the parking lots were too far for Shirley to walk from. She refused to stop at any restaurants because she wanted to go back to the same barbecue place we went to last week! Did I finally lose it at the end of this day? No, because she was leaving the next day!

"What time do we have to leave for the airport?" she asked.

"Well, your flight is at 3:30, so we should leave here no later than noon."

"Oh, no," she said. "That's too early. You know, I just get into a wheel chair at the curb and they take me right up to the gate."

"OK, but there's traffic, and possibly an accident, and you should be there a couple of hours before the flight leaves."

After prompting, cajoling, and pleading for her to get ready, she finally emerged from her room at 1:30. We did hit traffic, and an accident in the tunnel, and did not arrive at Logan until 3:30 p.m. I dropped her off at the curb; of course she missed her flight, but at that point I felt a surge of satisfaction that she was going to be quite inconvenienced!

She called a week later to tell me how horrible her journey home was. I was minimally sympathetic. "You know," she said, "next year I'd like to come back, but I'd want to be closer to the water."

"Oh, Shirley, I think you'd love Wellfleet. Call your travel agent and have her make arrangements. Oh, and be sure you let me know what weeks you'll be there." Because, I said to myself, I'll be sure to be absolutely unavailable!

Me and the Condo KGB

CONDO LIVING IS NOT for everyone. I was aware of this when my husband and I bought our first condo in N. Woodstock, NH. There are crazy neighbors, and rules and prohibitions which can outbalance the convenience of low maintenance. However, we had a great condo association, very fiscally sound and completely reasonable. We did live next door to some weird neighbors, but in as much as they drove everyone else crazy, they were nice to us. Maybe it had something to do with not wanting to go to war with people just a wall away. I sold the unit after my husband died and my cousin burned down the place – but that's a story for another day.

My second condo venture was in Coconut Creek, Florida. Technically it's part of Pompano on the east coast, but it's getting big enough now to have its own zip code. I bought it to winter there and to visit my son who had re-located to Ft. Lauderdale a few years earlier. This condo was a little different. It was an over-fifty-five complex with five thousand units, ten thousand residents. Actually, it was a small town all by itself with a health center, theater, workshops, ballroom, golf course, tennis, swimming, etc., etc. The grounds were gorgeous with flowering shrubs, fountains, palm trees, a lake. It was paradise. Almost.

I should have been a little suspicious when I was buying the unit and the condo regulations ran to over sixty pages of small print. Who has time to read all that stuff when you're in the midst of dealing with banks and realtors and furniture companies? The realtor told me the condo board was very lenient about rules. File that under "famous last words."

The first winter I was there, I immediately ran afoul of the condo board - who shall hereafter be referred to as the Condo KGB. I was walking across the lawn in back of my unit to try to get a better camera angle on the egrets who were regular visitors to my patio. Suddenly, a window opened in a building next door, and a woman shouted, "You're not supposed to be walking on the grass."

I shouted back, "What are you talking about?"

She continued, "It's in the condo docs. It's against the rules to walk on the grass."

Laughing and not at all intimidated, I said, "I don't care. I'm walking on the grass if I want to!"

A few days later, there was a note in my mailbox from the condo board that I was in violation of rule # 166 which prohibited residents from walking on the grass. This was a "friendly" reminder. Later that winter, I had a St. Patrick's Day party at the pool. Another notice appeared shortly after, informing me that there was no food or drink allowed at the pool. "How are we supposed to have a party without food or drink I inquired?" To that, I got no response to which I concluded one was not supposed to have a party at the pool. I had seen other groups partying at the pool, so my guess is the ones who complained were the uninvited!

The following year, I was cited for violating rule # 231 which states that residents are not allowed to have guests stay in their unit when said resident is not there. This infraction occurred because my step-daughter always came down to Florida the first week in December and stayed in the condo with her friend Jennifer. I typically would not arrive until after Christmas. "Are you telling me that a family member can't stay in a condo owned by another family member?" I asked incredulously.

"Well," my neighbors explained, "this is really for our benefit. You know, we just can't have people putting their places up on Home Away or Air B n B. Anyone could claim to be a relative, you know." I was wondering how any guest on either of those sites could be any worse than some of the wackos I saw parading around these premises. And, if I own the place shouldn't I be the one to say who stays there?

Then there were the cats. The condo rules state that there are absolutely no pets allowed in Wynmoor. However, there was a steady parade of dog walkers filing past my sidewalk every day. "If pets aren't allowed, how come these people are all out walking their dogs?"

"Oh, those are emotional support dogs," I was told. "You have to go to your doctor and get a letter stating that your pets are necessary to your emotional well-being, and then you can have them." If I went to my doctor and asked him for such a letter, I'm sure he'd tell me to get the hell out of there ASAP!

Sure enough, shortly thereafter, I got another letter from the condo board telling me I was in violation of rule # 15. I needed to have a letter on file from my doctor, and I was not allowed to have the cats leave my unit. The lady from the building next door was rapping at my door one morning, fuming about the fact that my cats were wandering around in her front yard. "No!" I exclaimed in horror!

"You know," she growled, "you're not supposed to let those animals outside. They frighten people!"

"Well," I said, "my cats are outdoor cats, always have been. However, I will speak to them, but you must understand, sometimes they simply cannot be compelled." At this, she concluded I was crazy and walked away quickly back to her own place. Yes, crazy always works! Regrettably, she continued to be my number one suspect when one of my cats mysteriously disappeared a few weeks later. I'm not saying she harmed it, but someone did report seeing animal control parked in front of her building one morning.

The following year, I changed the venue for the St. Patrick's Day party. I decided to have it at the tennis clubhouse. I got in touch with the president of the tennis club, cleared it with his board, and invited 35 people to a catered corn beef and cabbage dinner. It was the party of the season! Everybody stayed so late, that it was after dark when we were finally cleaning things up. So dark, in fact, that I tripped on the edge of the tennis court and sprained my ankle. It swelled up like a basketball, and I was lying on the couch with ice on it when there was a knock on the door: another notice from the condo board. It, seems I violated condo rules by not going through the condo board first for permission to use the tennis clubhouse for the party. Since they did not give permission, and I had an illegal party, they were fining me fifty dollars. I laughed because fifty bucks was pretty cheap for a party rental, and had I asked first, they probably would have said no.

Since buying the place in 2007, I had a running dispute with the condo board over the telephone. I did not have a land line telephone in my unit which was required by the emergency notification team. "I'm only here four and a half months a year. I have a cell phone. I don't want to pay a telephone bill for twelve months."

"You have to have a land line because that's how we reach you in an emergency. It's hard-wired into our system."

"Why can't you reach me by cell phone which is what the police do, and city hall does, and even the school department?"

"You have to have a land line because that's the rule."

This went on the entire eight years I owned the place. There was a running dispute involving other owners, mainly snow birds, who felt that a cell phone was sufficient. I knew several owners who did not have a land line phone. The younger buyers felt it was high time for the condo board to enter the twenty-first century. In the fall of 2014, I went for a two-week tour of the Baltics: Finland, Estonia, Latvia, Lithuania. I returned home to a mountain of mail and was aimlessly leafing through it when I noticed the return address of the condo board. This can't be good, I thought, and it wasn't. The gist of the letter said that since I had not complied with their request to install a land line telephone, the board had voted at their last meeting to fine me one hundred dollars a day for every day there was not a land line phone in the unit commencing November first, which was one week away. I laughed and said to myself, "That's ridiculous! They can't do that!"

The next day, I was telling my friend Linda about the crazy condo board letter, and she said, "I think they can do that. You need to talk to your lawyer." I called George. He was one of my several high school classmates who ended up passing the bar exam.

"June," he said. "Just put in the damn phone! Of course, they can fine you. I tell my clients that if they can only pay one thing a month, pay the condo fee, because the condo association has more power to take your property than the bank does! Oh, and if they do fine you, even for one day, that will go on your credit report, and you will probably never be accepted by any association again."

OK. Now I was really in trouble. I had to get a land line phone installed in a condo seventeen hundred miles away and in five days. My neighbors helped out by waiting for AT&T who canceled twice! Well,

AT&T finally installed the line but not a telephone. So, another neighbor went to Walmart and bought a cheap phone to plug into the phone jack. Then, I had to call the condo board and give them my new number, so they could call it and verify.

When I returned to Florida, the first thing I did was call Melanie, my realtor. The lock box went on, and the place sold in five weeks. A guy in my building, who was also on the condo board, asked if I was leaving because of that thing with the land line telephone. He phrased it as if that would be a silly thing on which to base a sell off. "Oh, no, Joe! Why would you think I'd take exception to my neighbors picking my pocket to the tune of a hundred bucks a day??"

When the new owner took possession, she discovered that the unit never had been wired for the emergency notification system. She had to cough up three hundred dollars to make that happen, but she didn't mind. The KGB had brainwashed her into believing that it was all for her own good.

Monday Night at the Death Café

A FEW WEEKS AGO, MY friend Betsy Mangan called to see if I could help her out with establishing some contacts in Sandwich for a new project she was getting involved in. She belongs to a national outreach group called Compassion Care, and its mission is to help terminally ill patients decide when to end their lives with medical assistance. They will tell you quite emphatically that it is not suicide because the person is already six months or less away from dying, and were they not already terminally ill, they would not consider ending their lives. She asked me if I was comfortable with the idea, or did I find it too gruesome to consider. I told her I had no problem with it. Anyway, without knowing too much more about the group, I went through my list of Sandwich contacts like the library, First Church, the A.L.L. speakers committee, the Unitarian Church of Barnstable, the Sandwich Women's Club, and the like.

We set up a date at the Sandwich Library on a Saturday afternoon at the end of March to hear a Dr. Kligler speak about the movement. He is the driving force behind the Cape and Southeastern Massachusetts chapters. Dr. Kligler is a very slender, gray-haired man, about 5' 10" tall, in his mid-sixties, and he is dying of prostate cancer which has metastasized throughout most of his body. He is soft-spoken, not by nature, I believe, but rather by the sheer effort of getting up out of bed, getting dressed, and driving a half hour or more to speak to a group of strangers who may or may not be receptive to his message. He starts out by telling us about his life before cancer, and his lifelong passion for medicine and his patients. His oncologists predict he has about seventeen more months of life. When he finished this narrative, I was not feeling sorry for him, but for the myriad patients who would no longer benefit from his care. Yes, he really is that compelling.

There are now eight states in the U.S. that allow end of life medical assistance, and the goal of the Cape group is to persuade the citizens and the legislature to make it legal in Massachusetts. The process for a patient who wishes to end his or her life is quite long and complicated. First, the person must have six months or less to live as certified by two physicians. A psychiatrist must attest to the patient's sound mind. There is an initial application, and then a waiting period. Only the patient can request this service, not family or friends. Finally, the patient himself administers the lethal dose, not the doctor. Oddly enough, only 2% of patients who apply for and get permission to do this actually go through with it. Maybe it's comforting just to know it's always an option!

I think it was a successful meeting at the library. There were about forty people in attendance, and they asked lots of questions. Most of them were retirees who wanted some options for not burdening their families with a prolonged and difficult end of life situation. Some were merely curious. Some were argumentative and raised the usual alarms about what could go wrong with this idea. I told Dr. Kligler after the talk that I was very grateful for his interventions because I had always planned to orchestrate the end of my life, but it would certainly be nice to have a little help and company!

If you want to be part of this movement, you can join a group that meets once a month in various locations and calls itself The Death Café. I am told the name originated a decade ago in Great Britain, but truthfully if the topic itself did not put me off, the term Death café definitely gave me pause. So, when Betsy called a few weeks ago and asked if I would like to be part of the education/entertainment portion of the Falmouth Death Café, I was a bit hesitant. "Tell me more about this," I stalled.

"Well," she said, "remember my short play 'Lost & Found' that we did in Sandwich in 2016? The one about my sister on Nantucket losing my mother's ashes the weekend before we were supposed to bury her in the new cemetery plot? I talked to Heather who runs the Falmouth Death Café and asked her if it might be an interesting idea to do my play after one of the meetings. There's always two parts to the meeting: first the round-table discussion and then the education/entertainment portion. The whole night runs about two hours."

"And you want me to do what?" I asked her.

"Oh, I want you to play the part of my older sister Pamela. It's on her property that mother's ashes went missing. Celeste Howe will be playing me, and I'll direct."

"Oh, OK. I hate to say this, but this Death Café performance could be fun."

"Oh, it will be," she said. "They're not morbid or anything, and they're very excited about the idea."

I got to the First Church in Falmouth early the night of the Death Café. The meeting was in the Fellowship Hall, and entering the room, I was greeted by a sign that said "Talking About Death Won't Kill You!" Thus reassured, I proceeded to sign in. The aroma was so tantalizing I wanted to take a bite out of the air. The Pastor of the church was in the kitchen baking brownies and cookies for the members. He does this all the time I'm told. I sat at a table of six other people, and after introducing ourselves, each person had a chance to voice concerns and experiences related to death – family members, friends, one's own death. Everyone there had the same basic belief - that it was time to consider our own demise. If we spend most of our lives learning how to live, doesn't it make sense to learn about dying? Of course, discussion of the passing of legislation to allow medically assisted death was like preaching to the choir. This group was in absolute harmony and celebrated the passage of the bill in the Rhode Island legislature that week.

Then, it was time to do our play. I was a little nervous about how it would go over with this crowd because it is a comedy and quite funny in places. More people had come in after the first hour, and we had about fifty people in the audience. They looked like they didn't know quite what to expect, but after a few minutes, the laughter came on a regular basis. Celeste and I had to hold back our lines several times to let the laughter die down. Enthusiastic, appreciative applause greeted the end of the piece. Whew! They liked it!

Betsy and I went out to celebrate at Liam Maguire's in downtown Falmouth. We toasted each other with Irish Coffees and decided that all things considered the Death Café turned out to be really fun! The next day, Betsy forwarded a text to me from Heather, the group leader. She wants us to go on the road! First to the Vineyard Library; then, the Day of the Dead Festival, and finally to the Death Salon at Mt. Auburn Cemetery to celebrate their new crematory!! We're thinking about it!

The Blizzard of 1978

I'M SHELTERING AT HOME during this pandemic of the Corona Virus, and it's reminding me of the Blizzard of '78. I don't know why that is exactly. First of all, this stay at home order came in the spring, and the blizzard was, well, in February, the dead of winter. This shut in experience has gone on for 9 weeks now, and maybe longer, and we were only sidelined for two weeks in 1978. I think what the two have in common is my attitude toward them. In both cases, I was perfectly happy to be home and at leisure. Of course, I wasn't stranded on Rte. 128 which became a parking lot for stuck cars, or sleeping in the lobby of the Howard Johnson Motel. I was teaching then at Shawsheen Tech, so I knew my paycheck wasn't in jeopardy.

We got two weeks off from school, and the town of Bedford, MA was a winter wonderland. I lived in a townhouse then, with a large parking lot. The snow piles were so high that we just dug snow arches to access the sidewalks. We were forbidden to drive in order to get the roads cleared. I remember walking to the supermarket and bringing groceries home on a sled. We didn't lose power; the house was warm and cozy, and the kids had a blast playing in the snow which got them really tired out and asleep early. I got to chat with neighbors I had never met, and caught up with those I only saw occasionally. Life was good!

One night into the second week of the stay at home order, my friend Peg called from the neighboring town of Concord. Her husband was stranded in upstate New York on business, and she was alone with the dog. "I'm going stir crazy here. How about you and David come over for supper tonight? I'll make chicken and dumplings, homemade bread, pie." Well, Peg was a fantastic cook, but there was a no drive order in effect. I hesitated.

"I don't know. We're not supposed to be driving."

"Oh, you're only five miles away. What are the chances of getting caught in that amount of time? I haven't even seen a National Guard truck anywhere in the past week."

"Yeah, I guess you're right. OK, we'll be over about five."

I got to work shoveling out the VW Bug which actually was great in the snow because the engine was in the back where the weight was really needed. In addition, if I did happen to get stuck in the snow, two guys or girls, could lift it up out of the rut. We piled into the car with my bottle of wine and David's games and puzzles. David was ten at the time, turning eleven in May. We drove leisurely through Bedford Center, deserted but so pretty with the street lights highlighting the snow on the Common.

Heading west on Rte. 62, we had just crossed over the town line into Concord, when I saw the headlights of a big truck behind me. "Oh no," I said, it's the National Guard." The truck pulled up next to me and indicated that I was to pull over. David looked stricken. "Are we in trouble?" he asked. "Are they going to arrest us?"

"I don't know. Don't say anything. Let me do the talking. OK?"

I pulled over to the side of the road, and a very tall guardsman walked up to the driver's side. Another soldier was standing in back of the car, taking down the license plate, I imagine. I rolled down the window. "Good evening, Sir."

"Ma'am, are you aware that there is a ban on driving in the state of Massachusetts?"

"Yes, Sir, I certainly am aware of that, and I would never break the law unless it was an absolute emergency." David is now looking like he might cry.

"And what exactly is your emergency, Ma'am?"

"My mother is all alone in her house in Concord because my father is stranded in upstate New York. He works for Polaroid, and they sent him there to set up cameras in a new RMV. My mother called to say she wasn't feeling well and could I please come over and help her with her medications." I was now pushing the bottle of wine under the driver's seat.

"I understand that, Ma'am. We'll be happy to follow you to your mother's house to make sure you get there safely."

"Thank you so much, Sir." Damn! This was in the day before cell phones. I couldn't even give Peg a heads up.

We took a road off Rte. 62, then another road on to Black Duck Pond, an idyllic spot with a cluster of 3 house built around a small pond, now frozen. The huge National Guard truck was behind us as I got out of the car and rang the doorbell. Now, I should mention that my friend Peg is eleven years older than I am, and that she has let her hair go naturally gray. As Peg stood in the doorway, I threw my arms around her and said in a very loud voice, "Mom, I'm so glad to see you. How are you doing? Don't stand here in the cold. Let's get you inside." Peg looked puzzled, but she went along with the script. "These nice guardsmen followed me to make sure I got here OK." I waved a thank you to the truck.

"Good night, Ma'am. Be careful on the way home tonight."

Once inside, I collapsed on the couch and told Peg the story of my encounter with the National Guard. She was not impressed with my story. I couldn't figure out why.

"Oh," she fumed. "I can't believe that they actually believed that I was your MOTHER!"

I explained that her gray hair probably saved us. Otherwise, I might be sitting in the State Police Concord Barracks until they figured out what to do with us. I'm not sure that overrode her indignation at the assumption of her age! Dinner was delicious, and we encountered no problems on the drive home. Peg still says the same thing, now, years later whenever we tell that story. "Can you believe they actually thought I was her mother???"

Lunch at the Barnstable County Jail

I'M NOT A GOOD person to let loose at a silent auction. First, I wander around checking out all the offering. Then, I start feeling bad for the items that have no bids or only one bid. Against my better judgment, I write down my name and a bid on the underserved treasures. This is what happened at the silent auction at the Sandwich Arts Alliance gala in August.

By the end of the night and several drinks later, I had forgotten which items I had bid on. Imagine my surprise when Mark Snyder announced that I had won the bid for lunch with the Barnstable County sheriff! I picked up the goody bag which contained several useful items: a mug, a hat, a keychain, water bottle, eyeglass case, shopping bag, and a certificate entitling the bearer to bring three people to the county jail for a tour and lunch with the sheriff. I was laughing when I asked, "So, who wants to come to the jail with me for lunch?" I figured there would be no takers. Immediately, several hands went up, and I actually had to narrow it down to the first two – Kathy Aubin and Pauline Tessein.

When I got home, I read the certificate again. I had to call Sharon, the sheriff's secretary, to set up a time in September for the visit. I had been to the jail on numerous occasions to pick up posters for the Arts Alliance, but I had never been farther than the lobby. Sharon said we each had to submit our name, address, and license number before the visit so we could be checked out before being allowed into the building. I was thinking this was overkill because what's one criminal more or less in a jail anyway?

Monday, September 16th, we arrived at the jail at 11:00 a.m. I could sense from the chatter and nervous laughter from Pauline and Kathy that there was some trepidation about actually going inside now that we were there. I was OK with the whole thing having worked for a year at the Billerica House of Correction in 2000. The sheriff was James DiPaulo who had gone to Malden Catholic with my husband John, and I suspect that was the reason I got the job teaching four afternoons a week, rather than any stellar qualifications on my part. It was a unique experience, but that's a story for another day.

We were buzzed inside by the officer in the office enclosure after proudly announcing that we had an appointment with Sheriff Cummings. Not the sheriff, but Sharon his secretary came out to greet us. We were taken down a long corridor with nicely appointed offices on each side: counseling services, the deputy assistant to the sheriff, Sharon's office. The sheriff's office was at the end of the corridor, large, with several windows overlooking the lawns, a huge mahogany desk, several comfortable leather chairs, couch, and more trophies and certificates of appreciation than I could take in on one visit. Sharon said, "The sheriff will be in soon, but meanwhile you need to leave your coats and purses here in the office. You can't take anything into the building with you."

Sheriff James Cummings is a pleasant looking man in his sixties, very fit, grayish hair, twinkly blue eyes, and an engaging smile. He actually seemed pleased to see us, although I imagine this was an interruption in his very busy day. We started our tour traversing what came to be miles of corridor. He was very patient about answering questions.

"How long have you been sheriff?"

"Since 1999."

"What did you do before that?"

"I was in the Massachusetts State Police for several years."

"Oh. Where?"

"Always here on Cape Cod."

"How many prisoners are here now?"

"385, but we can handle 500."

"Well, that's good news," said Kathy. "At least crime isn't that rampant on Cape Cod. Are there prisoners from other parts of the state here as well?"

"No, just Barnstable County."

"What about Dukes County?" I asked.

"It's very unusual that we would have someone from the islands, but if we're asked, we'll accommodate them."

Pauline optimistically said, "There really aren't any serious criminals here, are there? I mean, wouldn't they be assigned to someplace like Walpole?"

"The guy who killed Sgt. Gannon is in that area down the hall." Well, I guess that answered that question!

The prison was built in 2005, and it is state of the art incarceration. Everything is spotless. There are no bars anywhere. Everything is controlled electronically by a master control room. In this room are four officers who constantly monitor every inch of the prison. There are TV screens covering the walls. I know we have been followed every step of the way on this tour. A door never opens until the door behind you clicks shut. I said to the sheriff, "You must have some heavy- duty generators here because if you ever lost power, you'd be dead in the water."

"We have several, and there's no way anyone can get to them." I thought they might be underground, but he didn't elaborate.

The entire prison is comprised of pods. It sort of reminded me of the way college dorms are set up. There is an open space with tables and benches and maybe thirty to forty rooms around that common area. There is a raised enclosure for the officers on duty, and they can open and close doors from their control panels. We were standing in the enclosure and some inmates were cleaning the tables. There is access to an exercise area just for that pod, and each pod has its own space. This means that there is no general area where all the prisoners can congregate. This cuts down on fights, and if there is bad blood, an inmate can be moved to a different pod and never see his adversary again.

"Can they see us?" asked Pauline.

"No, the glass is tinted so we can see out, but they can't see in."

The more dangerous inmates were in smaller pods of 10 or 12 rooms. And the most dangerous, well, the sheriff didn't take us there.

We saw the department store. This is where prisoners leaving for court can get dress clothes. When they come back, they switch the dress clothes for prison jumpsuits. There is a dry cleaners with moving numbered racks that clean and press the clothes for the next wearer. There are a series of rooms that one must pass through before getting to the vans on the outside, and it's a complicated process of finger printing before leaving and upon re-entry.

I asked the sheriff what the rate of recidivism was at this prison. "Sixteen percent," he proudly reported.

"Wow. That is impressive," I said. "When I was working at Billerica it was something like 62%."

"Well," he added. "We do have that population we refer to as the frequent fliers!"

It was after twelve noon now and time for lunch. The sheriff asked if we would like to eat in the officers' dining room, or could he take us out for lunch. A very generous offer, but we didn't want to take up too much more of his time. "No," we said. "We'd love to have lunch here". The food in the dining room was buffet style, cooked by inmates under the supervision of a chef who could grant them a certificate of culinary proficiency upon their release. There was home made soup, roasted chicken and vegetables, salad, cheese pizza for the vegetarians, and chocolate pudding for dessert. It was tasty!

The sheriff's department does a lot of community outreach projects. We talked about some of them over lunch. In addition to the print shop, there's the highway cleaning; they can deliver and set up tables and chairs for events; there used to be a crew that set up huge tents that were available free of charge, but that got phased out due to the age of the tents! The sheriff reported that his retirement is not on the radar screen. He loves his job and intends to stay there.

We left the sheriff at one o'clock after collecting our belongings from his office. We sincerely thanked him for his time and for letting us experience a thoroughly enjoyable morning. Who knew that two hours in prison could be so much fun? Sharon walked us out to the lobby and said goodbye. Later, on the drive home, Kathy said, "Oh, we didn't get any pictures."

"And that," I said, "might have got us a few hours in one of those pods!"

Chappaquiddick – The Movie

THE PHONE RANG AND I looked at the caller's ID before answering: Boston Casting. Better pick up on this one. They always email events. A call is definitely more serious.

"Hi, this is Michelle from Boston Casting. Is this June?"

"Yes, Michelle, what's up?'

"If you're available, we have a small part for you in the movie Chappaquiddick. You would need to be in Peabody for a costume fitting on August 23, and commit to two full days in September, the 19th and 20th. Would that work for you?"

"Definitely. I don't have to audition for it?"

"No. We have your audition tape from STRONGER. They used that."

"Yeah. I didn't get that part."

"That's too bad. It was a good audition."

"I was robbed."

"You know, I hear that a lot."

On August 23rd, I was at a warehouse in Peabody, very bare-bones and industrial. The head of costumes was a tall, red-headed guy with a pony tail, wearing a very expensive-looking Scottish dress kilt and gillies.

"What's up with that?" I asked one of the assistants.

"You know that movie 'Four Weddings and a Funeral'? she asked. "Well, ever since that came out he's been dressed like the Scottish guy they had the funeral for."

Rob Roy swooped down on me. "So you're one of the Kopechne family friends in the funeral scene. Try on these dresses and let's see about a hat."

Four dresses later, he finally approved one. I picked out a black straw hat, and he said, "No, no, that won't do."

"Let me try it," I said.

"Oh, I was SO wrong. It's perfect. I like the little black clutch bag, and do you happen to have just plain black pumps at home?"

I assured him I did. "OK, then. Let's get you over to hair and make-up."

The woman ahead of me in the stylist's chair was having three inches cut off her hair. When it was my turn, the stylist lifted up my hair a few times, flipped it around and said, "I think your length will be OK. Come on the set the morning of the shoot with your hair already in rollers, so we just have to comb it out. No make-up, clean face."

The morning of September 19th, I'm driving down route 3 at three a.m. The email said to be at St. Barbara's Church in Woburn at 4:30 a.m. to be taken by bus to the set- the location of which is very secret, very hush-hush. There are NO other cars on the road, and the total blackness is eerie. Sometimes I can see the lines on the highway, and sometimes I can't, so I'm not sure what lane I'm in or if I'm in any lane at all.

At St. Barbara's, the parking lot is pretty full. If any normal people are out and about, they must be wondering if there's some spiritual revival happening in the town or maybe something apocalyptic. A big Peter Pan bus arrives, and we all board. Every woman has rollers in her hair and no make-up. The guys just look tired. I'm thinking, "Do I really want to do this? What if I screw up royally?" To counter the negative thoughts I start yoga breathing, and repeating to myself, "I'm really excited to be here. I can't wait to get started. This is going to be great!"

We get to the set which is in Winchester – the Church of the Epiphany. It is gorgeous, very English Cathedral-like, with a courtyard fountain surrounded by cloisters. It is and has been raining all morning. I sign in before being herded into the church hall. "Remember," we're told, "there are absolutely NO cell phones allowed on the set. We see a cell phone, and you're dismissed. Period."

There are already about a hundred people there. We line up for hair and make-up. One of the make-up people asks, "Are there some of you who can do your own make-up? We're going for a sixties vibe: heavy eyeliner, bright eye shadow, pale lipstick."

"I can," I volunteer. "I was THERE!"

There are six women doing hair. I take out my rollers before I get to the chair. Five minutes later, I have an up do under my hat and a make-up person comes by to check me out. "Really good," she says, "but too light on the lipstick. Darken it a bit." We are now free to wander down to the end of the hall where breakfast is set up. This is an amazing smorgasbord of pastries, eggs, sausages, bacon, cereal, fresh fruit, juice, coffee tea, mineral water. I load up a plate and look for a spot at one of the round tables, but before I can choose one, I'm waved over to a group close by. This happens all day. These people are absolutely the friendliest people on the planet.

I say "thanks" and sit down. They all introduce themselves and continue talking about what films they've worked in lately. "How about you?" they ask. I tell them this is my first time ever on a movie set, and with those words, I am adopted.

"OK. This is what you need to do. First, sit here or somewhere very near the door because when the director needs extra bodies for a scene, he'll just pop in and grab the nearest people. Raise your hand and volunteer for ANYTHING. Doesn't matter if you don't know what you're doing, you'll figure it out. Just do what you're told, don't argue, and try not to piss anybody off."

I find out that all of these people have real jobs, but somehow they're able to take time off when they get a call from casting. One guy is a trial attorney who was a child actor in New York, and whose claim to fame is that he was JFK Jr's roommate at Brown. I asked him how that was, and he said, "We were always in competition for the same stuff, and he always got the top spot, so most of the time I felt like killing him!" Another guy ran a talent agency in LA, but came back to Massachusetts when he was battling cancer. He's one of the priests today.

It is now ten a.m. We've been sitting around for five hours, talking, laughing. There's a big card game going on in one of the side rooms, gambling, money on the table. The breakfast buffet has been cleared away, and now the mid-morning snacks appear. Rob Roy, the kilted costume designer, comes in and asks, "Anyone one of you ladies want to try on cat's eye glasses? I just found some." I volunteer, of course. He looks at me with the bright, white glasses on and says, "Perfect. I love it. Come with me."

I am spirited away to the cloisters and placed in a group of three other people. Rob Roy grabs my purse and says. "No, that's wrong. I'll bring you a better one." There are huge bright lights everywhere and miles of cable and wires. We are told to look somber, but converse naturally while walking into the church. It seems simple enough, but they shoot it three times.

I'm now sitting at a different table, but the same friendliness in evidence. A young man, who looks a little ragged around the edges, asks me if I think he looks tired. I think he looks like something the cat dragged in. He tells me he's been up all night and the previous day in Lawrence, working on the film DETROIT about the riots in that city. He plays a National Guardsman, and he was jumping in and out of a tank all night. Now he's playing a reporter on this one. He also tells me they've changed the name from Chappaquiddick to BRIDGEWATER. "What's the story on this Kennedy guy?" he asks me. "I mean, he wasn't even there on that bridge, right?"

"Only if you're going in for revisionist history," I tell him.

There's a commotion in the center of the room, and a guy in sweats with a long pony tail, calls for everyone's attention. He introduces himself as the S.A.G. (Screen Actors Guild) representative on this film. There's some talk about a new contract and where to find him if there are any questions. Then he invites all the SAG members to get in line first for lunch. My table mates apologize for going ahead of me. "You're not SAG, yet?" they ask.

"No, but if I start working on a regular basis I'll think about it."

Another tutorial: "Oh, you can't just join SAG. You have to have three vouchers to join. Every time you have a speaking part, you get a voucher, so you'll have one after today. If you get a commercial, that covers all three vouchers. Then you can apply for membership and you're allowed to pay your $1600 in dues. That's for New England. In New York, it's around $3,000. But the pay is way better if you're union. Now see, today, if you were union, you'd get extra money because we're working in the rain. Same for snow, strong wind, extreme cold or heat."

"Who keeps track of all this?" I wonder.

"Oh, the SAG rep. That's why he's here. Extra pay too for working with animals, oh and that machine spewing fog in the church that's supposed to be incense – extra pay for that too. Hazardous chemicals. For cast and crew SAG is our best friend. For the director – his worst nightmare."

Unbelievable! Lunch is really good: chicken and vegetables or lasagna, salad, rolls, lots of dessert. I sit for another couple of hours after lunch before I'm finally called to do a scene with Mrs. Kopechne on the church steps. We need umbrellas. It's pouring. They are provided instantly, of course. Again, they shoot it three times, must be some magic number, and I wonder if it will end up on the cutting floor. That happens a lot, I'm told.

At my next group of table mates I'm with a group of twenty somethings who have been designated "The Beltway Buddies." They are the D.C. friends of Mary Jo. The assistant director comes in and calls for Mary Jo's friends to go to the courtyard for the next scene. The girls are still sitting there. I tell them to GO. They've just been called. "No, we're the Beltway Buddies," they explain. "And who's Mary Jo?" "It's a long story," I tell them, "but trust me, they want YOU! GO!" Gotta love those millennials!

It's now six o'clock in the evening. I have officially been on the clock for thirteen hours. Now we are all herded into the church for the funeral scene, about two hundred of us. I'm sitting behind the Kopechnes, but in front of Jason Clarke who's playing Ted Kennedy. This is the first time I've seen John Curran, the director. He seems to have about a dozen people doing his bidding. It's hot and humid in the church, and the make-up people really are running around sponging faces and dabbing on fresh make-up, just like in the movies. Oh wait, this IS the movies. The head of the hairdressers plucks me from my pew and says, "Come with me. I need to re-do your hair." She tells me it's coming down in the back and in this scene the back of my head will be quite visible. I'm impressed with this level of detail, but actually I've been observing it all day. The crew may be wacky looking with pink, purple or blue spiked hair, and crazy clothes, but they are complete professionals on the set.

We are in the church for two hours, next to the fog machine, sitting through the priest's eulogy and part of a mass. They actually got a real priest for this part. My seat mate asks me if I'm Catholic. "Yes, why?" He wants to know if it's customary at a Catholic funeral to have the casket on the altar. I tell him it's not, but the spot where the casket would normally be is the platform for the camera.

Finally, at eight thirty, we are told to get changed, give back our costumes, and put in our pay vouchers. I have been on the set for sixteen hours, the second eight at time and a half. I figure I'll be getting about $400 for the day. The bus is waiting to take us back to the parking lot at St. Barbara's. As I'm driving back to Cape Cod, I'm trying to process everything that happened. I made some new friends, laughed all day, ate too much, and pretty much had the time of my life. Would I do it again? Absolutely. It was a party. I'd even be willing to pay THEM for the privilege!

Sandstock: The Woodstock Anniversary Concert

In April of 2019, at a brainstorming session for the Sandwich Arts Alliance, someone came up with the idea of celebrating the 50th anniversary of Woodstock, 1969. The idea was to have our own Alliance musicians showcased - performing the playlists from the original concert. We would have the event on August 17th, mid-point in the original 16 through 18 days of '69. The 17th was a Saturday this year and perfect for a free, outdoor music happening.

I have to say, I was not immediately on board with this plan. First of all, it sounded like a lot of work, and second, I am so skeptical of outdoor events in new England in August. It could be 100 degrees or 50 degrees, torrential rain, hurricane-force winds, or deadly calm and a feast for all kinds of insects. Any of which could render null and void months of planning and capital outlay. However, my co-coordinator, Diane, came up with the idea that we name Rick Sharp as the Event Manager and minimize our responsibility for the project. Now, Rick was a professional photographer on the PGA Tournaments in another lifetime. He also was on the road with some big-name rock groups during his career. He knows how to set up sound, lights, organize, publicize, and motivate. All I had to do is convince him to take on this little project.

I called him a few days later and outlined the plan. "Rick," I enthused, "this is your THING. This is what you do best." He was immediately excited about it which made me a little nervous. "This is great," he said. "All the other celebrations that have been planned have fallen through. We could have the biggest crowd in the country. I'm thinking maybe 4 or 5 thousand people. My girlfriend has connections with the Boston Globe. I can get some radio stations on board. What's our budget? What are we selling tickets for, and where is this taking place?"

OK. Time to start curbing the enthusiasm. "Well, see, it's like this. We have an expense budget of $2300. We're using the field in front of the bandstand, and it's a free event. It's kind of our 'giving-back-to the-community' gesture for the summer. We're thinking maybe 4 to 5 hundred will show up." There was dead silence on the other end of the phone for several seconds.

"You're seriously telling me that's the plan?" he finally remarked. " How do we pay the musicians?"

"Actually, we don't. We've budgeted $600 as a kind of honorarium for them, but we need the rest for publicity, rental fees, posters, a banner, Facebook blasts, and Constant Contact. You'll be responsible for recruiting the musicians. They have to be Alliance members or willing to join, and everything that goes along with the music: set lists, sound, rehearsals, meetings. Diane and I will cover the logistics."

Rick decided to meet with the musicians every Tuesday evening for an hour or so. The first meeting seemed promising. Steve Resnick, who had been at Woodstock in '69, was eager to act as a consultant. That is, until he learned the date. "I'm going to be in Maine that weekend with my grandchildren," he explained. "But good luck, anyway." Rick threw out the suggestion that everyone come in some kind of period costume, 60's Hippie Chic. That was met with stony silence. Finally, a group spokesman came forward with "We'll wear whatever we goddam please!"

Rick described the meetings in the following weeks as "herding cats." There was some jealousy about the fact that Rick was in charge and not one of the musicians, but that was the idea. Had we picked one group over another, there would be hard feelings. This was a compromise.

I got to work on the venue. I called the Town Hall to reserve the field and the bandstand, but they told me they belonged to the school department. I called facilities director, Mimi Shorten who said I couldn't do anything until I cleared it with Little League. It took a while to track down the Little League President, but he assured me that they would be finished with the play-offs and there would be no problem. But the concession stand would be closed for the season. Oh,oh. There are two bathrooms in the concession stand that are vital to our survival! I asked if we could please have the bathrooms opened for the day, and he said he would take it up at the June meeting. I got back to Mimi with the news, and she issued me a school department permit for August 17th for a $50 rental fee.

Greg Polanik came up with a design for the poster. It was loosely based on the original, with the dove sitting on the bridge of the guitar and some fingers on the strings. Rick said, "Do you think someone will sue us? I mean that poster has to be trademarked." We all laughed and said, "We have no money. What will they recover if they do?" Anyway, we're calling it "Sandstock" not Woodstock, and all the information is different.

In the background while all this was happening, our development team went out and got us sponsors. Coca Cola of Sandwich donated a truck with 500 pieces of product that we could sell. Graziella's Artisan Pizza agreed to pay us $500 for the privilege of selling pizza that afternoon. A few smaller sponsors paid $100 each to sell carrot cake, ice cream, and face painting. I had written a grant for $500 from the Mass Cultural Council. It looked like we might be able to cover our expenses and break even, until Rick dropped the bombshell that the sound engineer we needed was going to cost $750.

Two weeks before the event, I still had not heard from the Little league about keeping the bathrooms open. It was vacation time, and nobody was reading emails. Rick said we need to order porta-potties. I gulped. "Nauset charged us $400 a piece for them at the gala last year! We don't have that kind of money."

"Check out United," he suggested. "They have them at Sagamore Beach, and I'm sure they're less than Nauset."

I got a deal from United – two for $352 including insurance. I still had not heard back from the Citizens' Police Academy about providing coverage for parking and crowd control, and the reason for that was they had been in contact with the chief of police. Suddenly, everybody was having second thoughts about the viability of Sandstock! Sandwich Police Chief, Peter Wack (yes, that's really his name) contacted me to say he believed we needed 4 patrol officers and a squad car at the field. I blanched! Five officers at $60 per hour times 4 hours equals way more than we have money for!

It took me a while to compose a response that would not offend the chief while strongly stating our case. If there's one person in town you do not want to piss off, it's the chief of police. I thanked him for his concern, but explained we were billing this free event as a family-friendly picnic in the park with great music. We were expecting 200-500 people tops, and everything would be wrapped up by 4:30 in the afternoon. "Well," he said. "Are you expecting 200 or 500 people?"

"It depends," I explained. "If it's a beautiful day, people will go to the beach. If it's a rainy day, they'll stay home. If it's somewhere in between, they'll come to the bandstand. My biggest fear is not having a good crowd after all this planning. "

"Let me think about it and get back to you," he said.

The Monday before Sandstock, August 12, I got an email from the selectmen's secretary, Diane Hanelt. "The selectmen have requested that you come to the meeting on Thursday evening to discuss the plans for Sandstock. They have not signed off on the event, and they will be making a decision on whether or not it can be held."

"What??? I have a permit from Mimi Shorten at the school department that was issued last April."

"The school department uses the playing fields and the bandstand, but they're on town land, and the selectmen have jurisdiction over the use."

Unbelievable. Five days away, and we might not be able to use the venue. I gathered Rick and Diane for a strategy session. "I think they're freaked out about the whole Woodstock connection," Rick volunteered.

"Do they really think it's going to be sex, drugs and rock 'n roll on the Sandwich fields?" I wondered.

Diane said she thought they were just trying to cover their bases in case things went south, as in, "Well, that's not what they told us when we gave them permission."

Summoned to Town Hall! Good grief. Thursday evening the three of us, dressed in our most conservative, solid-citizen outfits appeared in the upstairs hall. We each had five minutes to explain ourselves. Rick talked about music; Diane talked about community benefit, and I explained that the Woodstock Generation was now in its 70's, and most likely all the old rockers would be coming in walkers. It was about nostalgia, not mayhem, and it was an alcohol-free family event. Bud Dunham, the town manager, was cracking up and looked like this was the best entertainment a selectmen's meeting had offered up in years. Unfortunately, he was not making the decision.

At noon the next day, one day before Sandstock, Diane Hanelt sent me a document giving the Sandwich Arts Alliance permission to use the town land for Sandstock. One hour later, Chief Wack emailed me to say only one officer was required for the afternoon. The Little League president said "someone" would open and close the bathrooms, and the Citizens' Police Academy said they were sending four volunteers. All good news, but so very down to the wire.

Saturday, August 17th was a sunny, cool, 75- degree day. The only crisis of the morning was finding out the porta-potties had no toilet paper. About 400 people total came according to the police officer on duty. The kids chased balls, played corn hole; the dogs had a play date, and lots of people came in vintage 1969 attire. We sold love beads, peace signs, and flowers. Checking out the crowd, I wondered why on earth I ever found that look "cool."? Three of the selectmen showed up and insisted on putting money in the donation buckets, actually chased us down to do it! It turned out to be the celebration we said it would: good music, dancing, singing, a peaceful four-hour Summerfest.

I was on clean-up duty with a couple of my houseguests after everyone left, and there was really nothing to clean up! The barrels had been used, recycling had been used, and there was not a scrap of paper left on the field. This was definitely not Woodstock! Word on the street was that Sandstock had been a wonderful event, and could we do it again next year? There's talk of doing an 80's Revival Festival, or BeatleFest, but definitely SOMETHING next summer. We seem to have prevailed in the court of public opinion too, as the Sandwich Enterprise came out with an editorial the following week criticizing the town for not being clear about their protocols for use of town property. The Sandwich Arts Alliance was the poster child for the absurd runaround we had to endure in order to get the necessary permits we needed. Good to know somebody watches the televised selectmen's meetings! And, of course, in some perverse way, it's still fun to know that Woodstock and the generation that spawned it can still inspire fear and trepidation in the hearts of public safety officials.

The Plumbing Plays

IN FEBRUARY, I GOT a call from my colleague Patti Cassidy. We both are members of Playwrights' Platform in Boston, and we met when Patti was the director of Watertown Community TV. She was doing a monthly program called "Play Café" where local playwrights would put together a staged reading of their latest short pieces and do kind of an author talk afterward. It was fun, and of course hugely flattering to be asked to participate.

Last year when the Sandwich Arts Alliance did an evening of ten-minute plays, we included Patti's piece "What Mona Lisa Saw" – a monologue of musings by the iconic portrait ranging over several centuries. So, I know rather than giving a nod to any talent which she might suppose I have, she was basically just returning the favor.

"I have a proposal you can't say no to," she began.

"Really? Want to bet on that?" I laughed.

"Seriously. I just contracted with The Plumbing Museum in Watertown to do a play festival as part of their one hundredth anniversary celebration."

"There's a plumbing museum in Watertown? Do people in Watertown even know there's a plumbing museum?"

'Well, probably not, and that's why Sasha, the curator, wants to do this festival – to raise visibility in the community. Are you in?'

I had enough inventory of short plays to come up with a decent entry, so I said, "Sure. Why not." About a week later, Patti called back to say that she just came from a meeting with Sasha, who was adamant about making sure all the plays were about plumbing.

"What??? OK. Now I know you're pulling my leg."

"Actually, no. Oh, and one other thing, the title has to come from an article in one of the plumbing journals that Sasha will put on-line for everyone."

"There's a plumbing JOURNAL??"

"Definitely. Goes back to the late 1800's."

"How many people have backed out so far?"

"Well, a couple, but I'm still recruiting."

"Good luck with that!"

"So, what's the verdict?" she inquired.

"You know, I'm probably going to regret this, but I'm accepting the challenge, if for no other reason than it will make a good story for my memoirs."

"You don't do memoirs. You're a playwright."

"After this experience, I may be switching genres!"

Well, I didn't have any experience with plumbing or plumbers, but should that get in the way of coming up with a play on the subject? Certainly not. The only thing that I could remember was a breakfast conversation my husband and I had several years ago with a couple of doctors staying at our bed and breakfast in Bar Harbor. They were building their vacation home in the mountains of North Carolina, and they were complaining about the high cost of plumbing contractors especially.

The husband said, "When I got the bill for the work and looked it over, I said to him, 'You know, this is more than I bill per hour for an office visit!' And, he said, 'Oh, yes. It's more than I billed an hour when I was a doctor.' When you were a doctor?? He complained that he just got fed up with bureaucrats telling him how to practice medicine, mountains of paperwork, sky-high insurance premiums, ambulance chasing lawyers. One Friday afternoon, he walked out the door and never returned. Now, he's his own boss, makes a ton of money and plans to retire at fifty-five."

OK, I decided. I can use that. I took my title from an old journal article titled "The Fable of the White- Collar Recruit." Who's more white-collar than a doctor, after all?

Here's the synopsis: Grandma Cummings, an inveterate matchmaker, is desperately trying to find a husband for her favorite granddaughter, Sophie who is twenty-nine, a career woman and in no hurry to settle down. She has set her sights on her next-door neighbor's grandson, a doctor who has just returned to town after completing a residency at the Cleveland Clinic. Interrupting her conversation with the said doctor one afternoon, there is a racket coming from the basement where a plumber is attempting to locate and fix a mysterious leak. When he appears in the kitchen with the bill, Grandma is taken aback at the charge for services. The doctor remarks that the hourly charge is more than he bills at his office, wherein the plumber says, "It's more than I billed an hour when I was a doctor," and continues the career change story. Grandma then concludes that she has found a better match for Sophie as she very unceremoniously escorts the doctor to the door. She invites the plumber to tea, finds out he's single, and ends the play with, "Well, Mr. Moran, this could just be your lucky day."

The other catch with this festival was that we were essentially producing our own work which meant finding actors, a director, props. I knew several actors from my days at working with the Atlantis Playmakers in Burlington, MA, and if you can't direct your own ten-minute play, you should get out of the business. I met Sasha Parfenova at the Plumbing Museum on the Monday before the festival. I was amazed at how young she is. I think this might be her first job out of art school. The museum would be a good space to work in: high ceilings, good acoustics, and since my play was taking place in a kitchen, the sinks and washing machines on display would not be a problem. I was actually feeling nostalgic around the 1950's décor and the wringer washing machine.

July 12th and 13th arrived, and we had sold out houses both nights. This is not such an impressive feat when you consider that seating capacity is about seventy-five. There was no charge for the performance; expenses were covered by a grant from the Watertown Community Foundation. In addition to my play, there were four others, all of them amazingly clever, and of course- comedies. Could anyone really write a serious ten-minute play about plumbing? And, no, that is not a challenge I would want to accept!

One play was about Picasso moonlighting as a plumber in his early down and out days in Paris. Another dealt with out of work journalists who decided to switch careers. They called themselves "Andy's List" and knew nothing about plumbing, but only billed when they could actually fix something. Then there was Uncle Shank, loosely based on Uncle Scrooge, who was visited by the ghosts of plumbers past, present, and future. The ghost of plumbing future was, of course, a woman. And finally, there was a play about a Super Mario Plumber at a Halloween party.

At intermission, people wandered through the museum, reading the placards on the exhibits and even staying afterward to explore. Sasha's idea of raising awareness seemed to be paying off. Before the last show on Friday night, she came to each of us and handed us an envelope. Inside was a check for $300. I had no idea we were doing this for compensation. Apparently, there are some heavy hitters on the board of directors, companies like Kohler, Moen, Crane, plus several local big plumbing contractors. They liked the idea and wanted to contribute.

There is some talk of doing a festival in the space again at some point. I'd love to see it happen. Anyway, I guess the moral of this story is this: Always say yes to a crazy idea. It could just turn out to be one of the most fun experiences of your life.

DANGER!
I'VE BEEN THINKING

So, I've Been Thinking . . .

NOBODY EVER ADMITS TO being a bad driver. Who here thinks they're a bad driver? Raise your hand. See what I mean? You could be the Typhoid Mary of the highway and still think, "Wow. I'm a pretty good driver." Watch the news. Everyday someone drives into a barber shop or a restaurant or a convenience store. Are they bad drivers? Hell no! It was mechanical error. The gas pedal was suddenly where the brake used to be. How did that happen? Nobody knows.

I admit to being a bad driver. It's true. I don't enjoy driving; I'm not good at it. I own up to it. Hey, there's a lot of things I'm really good at, driving doesn't happen to be one of them. I can live with that. But, I've never had an accident. Swear to God, never! Of course that doesn't take into account how many I've caused. The trick is – just keep going. Don't stop. Never, NEVER look back!

Sometimes people are really understanding about it. I backed into a car at a gas station last week. Just a tap, but I jumped out, apologized profusely, and the people were OK with that. I just wonder why they were writing down my license plate number as I left. Oh well. And another time I was pulled over by a state cop for exceeding the speed limit on route 6. I had a bumper sticker on my car that said: "English teachers are novel lovers." He asked me if I was a teacher. I said yes. He said, "What grade?" I told him high school. "OK, lady, you can go. Anybody who teaches high school has more than enough problems as it is." And that was nice.

Sometimes I can live in a place where my bad driving isn't an issue, like Florida. In Florida, bad driving is an art form. Six or seven lanes of traffic in both directions on I-95, and nobody's too sure about what exit is theirs. Why should they be? They're just visiting. They don't know where they're going. Stop signs? Why bother? The other guy's got brakes – maybe. And BIG cars: Lincolns, Cadillacs, Hummers. The rule of thumb in Florida is: the bigger the car, the smaller the person driving it! They're sitting on a booster seat, eyes just clearing the steering wheel. Of course I was a new comer too. I had to rely on my GPS most nights just to find my way back to my house. One night, my GPS tried to kill me. Seriously! She said, "In 100 feet you have reached your destination on your left." I looked left. There was a canal. In Florida, canals have alligators. That's how I know my GPS was trying to kill me.

Now I live on Cape Cod and once again I can get lost in a sea of bad drivers. Take Rt. 6, a virtual how to for bad driving. Especially in the winter. Nobody, but nobody ever does the speed limit. What's a speed limit? Most people are going 75 in the travel lane. In the passing lane it's 85, and the only time someone in the passing lane pulls over is when a state cop is coming up behind at 90 or 95! In the summer, it reverts back to kind of what Florida is like. Nobody knows where he or she is going, intersections are like Dodgems, cars are doing 15 in a 40 mile zone looking for streets that somehow have misplaced their street signs.

But I think being a bad driver kind of helped me on my first summons for jury duty. I was called to the Cambridge Court House to hear a drunk driving case. I tried to explain to the judge that my lack of expertise as a driver might disqualify me as a juror, but she wasn't buying it. So, there we were in the jury room deliberating the facts of the case. A man in Wakefield, MA, on a sunny afternoon in June, in his own neighborhood, veered off the road, drove over his neighbor's lawn and wiped out the front porch. He pleaded not guilty, but did admit to drinking a couple of beers with lunch. My fellow jurors immediately concluded that he was guilty of OUI. But I said, "No. It could happen. What if he dropped his ice coffee and reached down to pick it up, or a bee flew in the window, or he lost control of the car trying to avoid a runaway puppy? " These were all things I had experienced. But, in the end, we did find him guilty. I hope we were right. Because if he were just a bad driver, like me, what he really needed was understanding, oh, and a really good insurance company!

What Could Go Wrong?

MY COUSIN LISA'S DAUGHTER is planning to get married in the summer of 2019. We all had lunch together a few weeks ago, and Morgan outlined her plans for the big day. These included a July, outdoor wedding, in a meadow near the ocean in a place called Fortune's Rocks, Maine. Her mother and I pointed out that New England weather can be capricious at best, and nightmarish at its worst.

"But, we'll have a big tent and fans in case it's hot or rainy. What could go wrong?" Morgan, with the optimism of youth, asked.

What could go wrong indeed? I've been to a few of those outdoor weddings, and the answer is: Everything! First of all, even with fans, on a sunny day those tents can heat up to 90 degrees or more. If it's a rainy day, anyone sitting on the fringes of the tent will get soaked. If it's not a rainy day, but it has rained the day before, guests will be slogging through mud to get to the tent which may or may not have a carpet of straw. As the reception slides closer to evening, the bugs will be uninvited guests. Did I forget to mention the ticks that are probably lurking in that lovely meadow? The predominant perfume of the day has to be Eau de Deep Woods Off.

Even with the best laid, very conservative, traditional plans, things can go wildly awry. A cautionary tale is my second wedding to John Barrett. Because we met on Halloween, John wanted to get married on that day. That being a bit too weird for me, we settled on the Saturday closest to it, at the Irish American Club where we both belonged. A late fall evening, crisp cool weather, I envisioned candle lit lanterns on each table, and a fire blazing in the hearth.

The first glitch was the guest list. Of the 200 invitations sent, only 165 had RSVP'd by the week before the wedding. We debated how to handle this, and settled on a number of 180 for the caterer who assured us he could ramp up the buffet supper if more guests actually arrived.

Next was the debate over whether or not to have an open bar. This "debate" almost derailed the wedding. I voted for, John voted against.

"We can't have an open bar," he explained, "because your cousins are heavy hitters."

"OH!" I sputtered. "My cousins??? And your family is on the wagon suddenly??"

This finally got settled by putting a dollar amount on the bar, after which drinks would not be free.

Then, there was the wedding cake. I spent several years teaching at a technical high school which had an amazing culinary arts department. Gary Levin, the department head, volunteered to make the wedding cake when he heard the news.

"Do you want me to deliver it to the Irish American Club?" he asked.

"Oh no, Gary, we'll pick it up Friday afternoon." I didn't want to impose any further on his generosity.

Friday afternoon, November 2, was unseasonably warm. Actually the temperature climbed to 80 by the afternoon. We put the cake in the hatch carefully, but got stuck in traffic due to an accident on Route 3. The frosting was beginning to soften in the warmth of the car, and every time we took a corner, the layers slid a bit. By the time we got to the Irish American club, the cake resembled something akin to the Leaning Tower of Pisa. We tried to push the layers back into place, but succeeded only in smudging the frosting.

The next evening, the temperature was still unseasonably warm. I didn't need a coat. Instead of lighting the fireplace, we were trying to re-start the air conditioning. People kept blowing out the candles in the little lanterns because they believed they gave off heat!

The cake, ensconced on a little table at the end of the buffet table, leaned precariously to the right. John and I cracked up when we saw it, and guests were fascinated. A few actually came up to me and asked if I minded if they took a picture of it.

"Of course not," I told them. "I think it's a hoot."

Mossy Coughlin and his band had just started playing when Mossy spotted the cake. He stopped in mid-song and announced, "Ladies and Gentlemen, I want to call your attention to this very EYEtalian cake here. A little bit of Italy comes to an Irish wedding!"

Half way through supper, the caterer came to us and said we have to cut the cake NOW because in another few minutes it's going to topple over!

By the time we got to the first dance, Mossy had been to the bar a few times, and was feeling puckish. So, John and I danced to "Please Release Me, Let Me Go". I had asked Mossy to please keep the decibels down because we had many senior citizens who were not receptive to loud music. For the first part of the evening, the band was pretty sedate, but by ten o'clock, Mossy was rockin'.

All in all, it was a pretty good party as long as everyone maintained a healthy sense of humor. The point here is: Man plans; God laughs. Even the best laid plans take on a life of their own, so never, but never be so bold as to tempt fate!

I'll Drink to That!

EVERY DAY I RUN into someone who tells me that they don't like the term "old" or "senior" or "elderly." I just laugh and tell them it's not a problem for me. I love being old. I wake up in the morning happy that I'm old. I don't remember waking up in the morning when I was young and thinking, "Wow. I'm really glad I'm young." Maybe I've just learned the virtue of gratitude, and I'm grateful for every good thing in my life, including my life!

Anyway, what was so great about being young? I did not have a wonderful childhood. I can remember spending most of it wishing I were not a child, and that I could make decisions for myself about where I lived, what I could do, how I could form my future. Things picked up a bit in high school, and by college life was glorious, the best four years of my life. Then, there was a real plateau in my life satisfaction quotient that coincided with having to work for a living.

Do I long for the days of rising at five in the morning, going out in the freezing cold at six to drop the baby at the sitter's, arriving for work at seven fifteen after only four hours of fretful sleep after a night with a colicky baby? NOOO! Do I miss working all week and spending weekends shopping, cleaning, cooking, washing, ironing, correcting papers? NOOOO! And then there was the money. What money? At a time in my life when my expenses were the highest, I was ironically earning the least amount of money in my career. A car repair could trigger a panic attack. I'm remembering all the days I went to work sick because like all working mothers, we had to save our sick days for when the kids were sick. Did being young make up for all of that? NOOOO.

Then, there was the problem of not being taken seriously because you're young, of having your opinions discounted because you're young, of being passed over for promotion because you're young, and it's not your turn. People also had the crazy idea that because you were young, you could work longer, harder, handle more problems, need less sleep. Not true. I got tired, stressed, discouraged in the same way then as I do today. I spent my twenties and thirties being sleep deprived.

Middle age brought a reprieve from the worst of the deprivations of the previous decades, but consider this: menopause coincides with teenage children, husbands with mid-life crises, and aging parents. Does anyone ever say, "God, how I long for those glory days of middle age?" I don't think so.

So, now I'm old. Considering the alternative, that's not a bad thing to be. And, there are perks, lots of them. Discounts for seniors on practically everything. Money gets deposited into my checking account every month and I don't have to go to work, a miracle which most of civilization never got to experience. My health is good, and when it's not, I can stay home and recover at my leisure. I don't have to short change my recuperation for the job. I do things a bit slower now, but who considers the energizer bunny a heroic figure? I don't know where my alarm clock is, and I never make an appointment before ten o'clock. On the odd day when someone calls a meeting for 9 a.m., I feel no obligation to be dressed in anything but my pajamas. Eccentricity is another perk of old age!

And, I play the age card. Flagrantly! I used to play the widow card, but after about ten years that gets old. Now, if I don't want to go somewhere I say, "Oh, it's just so far, and night driving at my age!" Of course, I regularly drive to Virginia to visit the kids, but that's not common knowledge. My age can be the catch-all excuse to escape doing almost anything. My favorite is, "I'm seventy-five years old! What do you expect from me?" Other problems just disappear when you're old. Take, for instance, the ME TOO movement. Sexual harassment takes on a whole new perspective. If a bunch of construction workers are cat-calling out to some sweet young things, I'm on the sidewalk shouting, "Hey, over here, ME TOO!"

Many people drag out that old cliché "I'd love to be young and know what I know now." I can't comprehend what kind of lives they've led, but I pretty much knew everything I needed to know for the time I was in, and the world changes too fast to rely on most past experience anyway. I do know that when someone refers to me as "elderly" or even "old," I just want to join them in a drink and celebrate!

What's Love Got To Do With It?

I'VE REALLY TRIED ALL my life not to be so rude as to eavesdrop on people's conversations, but with everyone yakking on cell phones in check-out lines, elevators, and even bathroom stalls (!), it's impossible to tune them out. There is one thing common to almost all phone conversations. It seems today everyone ends a call with "I love you." How did this get started? What happened to "good bye"? Is this the new "Have a nice day" inanity?

I'm always uncomfortable hearing the phrase "I love you" from a stranger, as if I should somehow fade into the background and be invisible to this intensely personal information. The thumb flexing, speed dialing generation seems to be oblivious to any incursion of privacy though, so maybe it's a youth thing, right? Not so fast.

Suddenly, my ninety- year-old aunt Ruth ends all her conversations to me with, you guessed it, "I love you." I have been her favorite niece since I was born. She is the closest thing to a fairy godmother anyone could have; she's my second mother. Never for one second of my life did I ever doubt that she loved me. Now, she has to reassure me every time I pick up the phone?

My parents didn't go around telling me they loved me. It would never have occurred to my John Wayne type dad that such a thing was necessary or appropriate. "Talk is cheap," he used to say. "Empty words," my mother would echo. The message was: if you wanted to let someone know how you felt about them, show them. Your actions spoke much louder than your words. They worked hard at being good parents, good providers. They lived love; they didn't talk about it.

So, I find this constant need to reassure someone that you love them odd. First of all because love, to me, is an action word – better show than tell. Also, the more you use an expression, the less meaningful it becomes. Things that are special are rare, not commonplace.

Someone once told me that the Inuit people have forty-one different words for the expression of love. Maybe that's the result of six months without sunlight and lots of down time in the igloo, but they seem to be on to something missing in our abbreviated lingo. The Greeks had different expressions for erotic love, familial love, love of country. So what are we really saying when **we** use the word love? Do I love you the way I love chocolate, or summer on the cape, my mother, or the color purple? Until we come up with some more specific expressions to categorize affection, I can only suggest that instead of saying "I love you" all the time, maybe you could just take out the trash.

Now, you're probably getting ready to ask, "What's WRONG with saying I love you to people you care about?" And my answer is – nothing! But when we over-use any expression or symbol it begins to trivialize it. It lessens the power of the words, and to me, that's quite sad. Just sayin'.

Do Not Go Gentle Into That Good Night...

(Dylan Thomas)

EVERY DAY NOW, IT seems some group springs up and announces a march- flashlights illuminating passionate placards to "Take Back the Night." To all of them, I say, "Don't take back the night! Leave it where it is!" Man was not made to traipse casually through the blackness of night. Do we have glow-in-the-dark eyes? Is our food supply most accessible after nightfall? Do our bodies absorb vitamins from the moon? We have been seduced by a small, but insidious conspiracy of insomniacs into believing that the night will unfold the mysteries of life if only we stay conscious long enough to experience it.

Who are these lunatics? The first was undoubtedly a cave dweller. Moonstruck, he wandered away from the comfort of the cave fires into the abyss of the night. His bones were recently unearthed from a riverbank by enthusiastic archaeologists in France. The bones of the rest of the family were found where they belong- ritualistically piled in a burial cave adjacent to the living quarters. Archaeologists later discovered this anomaly which seemed to occur with chilling regularity during the entire Pleistocene Period.

The Egyptians were an enterprising lot whose chief deity was the Sun god. Primarily an agricultural people, they made hay while the sun did shine. Naturally, they were reluctant to release the Israelites into the hands of a god who commanded his followers to run amok in the middle of the night smearing doors with the blood of slaughtered animals! And, for their midnight foray out of the land of the pharaohs, the Israelites won a forty-year stint in a sand trap resembling Phoenix before sprinkler systems, or worst- case scenario, the only land in the Middle East without oil.

The Romans invented the sundial so people could keep appointments in the daylight hours. They believed the night air contained unhealthy humors (as anyone who's been to a comedy club can confirm), so they wore elaborate head scarves to ward off unseemly vapors. During the ides of March in 49 BCE, a small group of insomniacs wandered from portico to portico plotting the assassination of Julius Caesar, an event best remembered by William Shakespeare who finally assembled all the details some sixteen hundred years later.

Eventually, the Romans abandoned the Etruscan work ethic in favor of elaborate night revels (also known as orgies), threw off their head scarves, and consequently were decimated by barbarians who believed in getting a good night's sleep. After the barbarians torched everything flammable in the city of Rome, Europe found itself immersed in the Dark Ages. The one bright spot in this dismal landscape was the work of the monks illuminating manuscripts. This began a tradition of literary criticism that continues today where everyone has an opinion of what the writer actually meant.

The Renaissance signaled a new celebration of daylight. Poetry extolled the pastoral; music banished darkness and brooding; canvasses explored the properties of light. Landlords all over France were getting top dollar for lofts with skylights, which were exempt from rent control. The celebrated playwrights of the English stage saw their productions performed at the Globe theater in natural daylight. As soon as some insomniacs tried to pervert that tradition by performing at night by torchlight, some left-over gremlins from the Dark Ages re-surfaced and burned the theater to the ground.

However, the Renaissance was not without its somber interludes. Louis the XIV, known as the Sun King, really wasn't too bright. The Borgias finally succeeded in poisoning everyone of importance, and the Medici invented divorce Italian style. The Reformation obsessed over Hell, a place pretty dark and dismal for all its fire and brimstone. All of this took a terrible toll on artists, and for the entire 18th century, no one could think of anything original to do, and so copied everything previously dug up from the ancient Greeks and Romans whose luminescence has been previously discussed.

The arrival of the Romantic Period signaled the beginning of the end. Suddenly, odes to nightingales, ravens, and bats appeared. The Germans were fascinated by compacts made with the devil. Melancholia became a national pastime. Herman Melville popularized whale hunting which resulted in a glut of oil on the world markets. This made it possible for an entire generation of insomniacs to burn the midnight oil.

Finally, in the 20th century, insomniacs made an all-out bid to dominate world culture. Electricity begat neon signs, which begat gambling casinos, which begat all-night entertainments which begat armies of journalists reporting on each other's coverage of the former. Not since the last presidential campaign had so much been said about so little.

The world is full of nocturnal creatures designed to fight, hunt, and feed by moonlight. Man is not one of them. It isn't natural. When man is about at night, he's likely a peeping Tom, a burglar, a gangster, a gambler, a drunk, serial killer, mugger, drug mule, or a member of the auxiliary safety forces created to deal with him in this darkened state. There is the occasional, legitimate night owl, the scientist or astronomer who must observe by dark, and true, you can only see grunion run under the stars, but really for the rest of us, I implore you, do not go gentle into that good night. Stay home!

In Search of the Magic Bullet

I WENT TO AN AUTHOR talk night a couple of weeks ago at the Sandwich library. The Sandwich Arts Alliance sponsored the event which featured four local writers: one non-fiction writer, one short story/novelist, and two playwrights. There were two playwrights because the other panelist, Bill Burbank, also a non-fiction writer, was hospitalized with pneumonia and died unexpectedly a few days later. R.I.P. Bill, and congrats on having an iron clad excuse for backing out of the panel.

I was, I think, more interested in the audience than the panelists. Who makes the effort at six o'clock on a freezing cold January night to come out and listen to a group of writers? Five people fought traffic all the way from Plymouth, and I recognized a couple of local poets and visual artists, but the rest were complete strangers. All of them were hoping to find, after the panelists finished speaking, that one suggestion, that one habit that would make it possible to join the ranks of bona fide writers, also known as "the magic bullet."

I hope they weren't too disappointed, but I'm sure that magic bullet never materialized. Having listened to the writing habits of scores of authors over the years, the conclusion I've reached is that one's writing process is as individual as a fingerprint.

Christie Lowrance, who wrote a biography of Thornton Burgess (Schiffer, 2013), started her career as a journalist. She researches, interviews, double fact checks everything, and sticks to a strict chronology of events in her writing. She is now working on a biography of George Bass, a nautical archaeologist. She writes in stages, first just collecting information, later fashioning an interesting narrative that will engage readers.

Carolyn LeComte writes everything fictional: children's books, novels, short stories. Her inspiration as a young child came from TV westerns. At the age of eight, she started writing episodes of GUNSMOKE and THE

LONE RANGER. What she loves most about writing is the element of surprise. She said she never knows where a story is going or what a character will do until it actually appears on the page. No, she does not plan a plot in advance, but she does write character sketches now to keep all the characters in the book consistent with their original descriptions.

The playwright, Karen McGarr, started writing skits as a child with her cousins to entertain at family parties. She's always kept a journal, which morphed into a blog called "Miss McGarr's Diary" read by over a thousand people a day worldwide. Everything she writes comes from her personal experience, and every day she sees a new play in some situation she encounters. Her play is pretty much formed in her mind before she ever sits down to write it, and so, there's never the terror of the blank page.

Betsy Mangan, another playwright, also relies on personal experience for her plays. She knows what she's going to write before she begins, and she is the only writer who talked about extensive revision. Once the piece is completed, she gets feedback from friends, playwriting groups, and family. Sometimes, what emerges is a very different story than the one she originally intended to tell. She does not write every day, but waits until she gets an idea and then runs with it. Then, she writes only on days when she's inspired to do so.

So, the golden nugget in all this is that if your process is in any way similar to any of these writers, VOILA! You're a writer. Even famous writers differ widely in their advice on how it's done. I looked up some quotes about writing online, and came up with these gems.

> "Writing books is the closest men ever come to child-bearing." - **Norman Mailer**

> "The purpose of a writer is to keep civilization from destroying itself." - **Albert Camus**

> "You never have to change anything you get up in the middle of the night to write." - **Saul Bellow**

"If you don't have time to read, you don't have the time (or tools) to write. Simple as that." - **Stephen King**

"Revising a story down to the bare essentials is always a little like murdering children, but it must be done." - **Stephen King**

"A professional writer is an amateur who didn't quit." - Richard Bach

"I believe myself that a good writer doesn't really need to be told anything except to keep at it." - **Chinua Achebe**

"Write drunk. Edit sober." - **Ernest Hemingway**

And a note on process: both Hemingway and Thomas Wolf liked to write standing up. Wolfe used the refrigerator as a desk, and Hemingway began writing after the bars closed. Hemingway also liked to write nude. Did you know that? No, actually, I just made that up to see if you were still paying attention. But, he always had cats hanging around the Key West house, and they were naked. So, what does that tell us? There's an element of truth in every rumor.

The Committee...
(or How to Get Published in 2019)

IT WAS A DAMP spring day in 2019 when Sam Moderato, editor of *The Swamp Land Review* – a self-proclaimed boutique literary magazine focusing on excellence in the creative endeavor – convened his panel of three selection committee readers. The submissions this year were numerous, and if they were to be ready for publication in the fall, there was a long, deliberative, work-week ahead.

After thanking them all in advance for accepting this challenge, Sam proceeded to the first story on the list of possibilities. "I imagine you've all had a chance to look at 'The Year Without Spring' which I rather enjoyed as an interesting coming-of-age story. The young man, Brian, makes his town of Carrick Fergus on the Irish coast into a pivotal character as the story unfolds in a rather James Joyce style of narration. Yes, Alisa?"

"Well, it's a young MAN'S story isn't it? Haven't we had enough of that point of view? I'd like to see a young woman's coming-of-age story. Why aren't we aggressively nurturing young female writers with a feminist viewpoint about growing up in America?"

Alex, while not in agreement with Alisa, had his own problems with the story. "I'm having difficulty with the lack of environmental concern in the part about Salmon fishing in the Shannon River. In addition to that, the pollution pouring into that river unchecked will ultimately affect the water quality of the residents as well as marine life in the sea. It seems irresponsible of the writer to blithely overlook those facts in his memoir."

"Now," interrupted Sam, "I'm not sure a teenage boy would necessarily have those concerns uppermost in his mind when teenage hormones were flooding his consciousness. However, I see Samantha more than ready to weigh in over there."

"There are so many things wrong with this story, I hardly know where to begin. As Alisa pointed out, it's Ireland. There are more Irish in America than there are in Ireland for God's sake! How does that contribute to diversity in America? And, they're CATHOLICS! Don't even make me go there! Minorities and under-represented populations, that should be our focus. Now if the writer were Ethiopian, living in Ireland as a child and coming to America as a gay teenager, that would be an interesting perspective."

"Thank you, Samantha," Alisa chimed in. "Where is the representation of the LGBT community? There is not a mention of any sexual orientation other than male heterosexuality. Are we supposed to believe no one in that community was gay, or trans-sexual, or bi-sexual? That's too much of an oversight for me."

"Why has no one picked up on the fact that animals were exploited in the anecdote about his grandfather's horse racing business?" asked Alex. "That's hardly the message we want to be sending to readers."

"Do we want to be sending messages to our readers? And, I'm not sure anyone saw it as exploitation then," suggested Sam. "Should we be judging 20th century norms by 21st century standards? I think we need to evaluate a piece in the context of the time it was written."

"I just think that's morally irresponsible," huffed Samantha. "We have a platform here to change minds and promote a set of values consistent with our principles and beliefs."

"Isn't that kind of the definition of propaganda?" queried Sam.

A resounding chorus of "no's" greeted that observation. "So, I feel the consensus is that we scrap 'The Year Without Spring'," Sam concluded a bit curtly. "I did think it was a charming piece overall. Well, on to the next story – 'A Jungle, A Soldier, A Village' which is a Viet Nam vet's story about a bonding experience coaching a kids' soccer team in the jungle. I liked the fact that the writer was able to transcend the horrors of war and focus on a common interest, namely a love of sports. Any thoughts on this one? Alex?"

"Was anybody bothered by the fact that some of the jungle cleared for a soccer field was probably defoliated using Agent Orange? That chemical made by Monsanto caused irreparable harm to all sides in the conflict. I don't see how that can just be glossed over. People need to be reminded that these companies profited from the war and were never held accountable for the deaths they caused. I mean if you're going to accuse other countries of chemical warfare, you better hold up a mirror first."

"I think the intent at the time was a dependable and thorough herbicide, not the execution of chemical warfare," explained Sam.

"Oh, so there's no guilt associated with unintended consequences?" added Alex. "I don't buy it."

"Oh," groaned Samantha. "Here we go again with a piece told by the conquerors! I'm sure the Vietnamese felt they were just pawns in another game of Colonialism. Would this be a different story if the narrator were female and Vietnamese? There can be no friendship with an invading army, only fear, loathing, and forced cooperation for survival. Anyone who believes otherwise is delusional as I believe this author is."

"These woman and children in that village were victims, VICTIMS!" shouted Alisa. "Sexual assault was rampant during wartime. Who's going to speak for them— the terrorized, the repressed, the tortured?"

Sam looked a bit confused. "Where in the story does it talk about sexual assault, or any kind of assault at all? Seems to me everybody was just trying to make the best of a bad situation in a world over which they had very little control."

"That's exactly my point," continued Alisa. "It's not mentioned. Another attempt by a bunch of soldiers to chalk it all up to 'boys will be boys'. What's needed here is a Me Too movement in Southeast Asia, safe spaces to come together as feminists to heal from eons of male subjugation."

"I really think you're reading way too much into this story," opined the editor. "It's a moment in time, an attempt to pull a wildflower out of a mound of mud. It's really beautiful in its simplicity and humanity. But, raise your hands if you're voting no."

Three hands shot up into the air. Heaving a deep sigh, Sam produced the next manuscript. "OK," he began, "this one is called 'Unbended Knee,' and it's the story of a transgender Mohawk Indian woman who was forcibly removed from a reservation in upstate New York to a private, boys' school in New England where he/she matriculated to Yale and received a master's degree in eco biology. Traumatized by this experiment in social equality, he/she then entered counseling to establish a true gender identity. As the story opens, she has taken a leave of absence from Green Peace to join a rodeo and expose the exploitation of animals used in these shows. However, before much evidence can be gathered, she encounters several episodes of unwanted attention of a sexual nature from the cowboys with whom she competes. Her dilemma now is: does she continue with her original plan, or drop everything to pursue sexual harassment charges against her employers? The pros and cons of this decision unfold as she narrates her stream of consciousness."

"OMG!" shrieked Alisa, "I love it. It spoke to me as nothing has in several months! Powerful, moving, and TRENDING!"

"Total agreement with that," gushed Samantha. "The ultimate in under-represented populations."

"I wish there had been more focus on Greenpeace," Alex weighed in, "but overall, it's a yes for me."

"Did we want to discuss the quality of the writing? It's a bit rough in places and downright obscure in others," commented Sam.

"Well, you're the editor, Sam," replied Alisa, "so edit it!"

Sam Moderato looked at his watch and wondered if it he could really start drinking at 10:00 a.m.

June Bowser-Barrett

About the Author

June Bowser-Barrett (B.A, M.Ed., M.A. The University of Massachusetts) is a former high school teacher, community college writing instructor, and gender equity consultant for the Massachusetts Department of Education. She began writing seriously when she stopped correcting reams of student writing.

Bowser-Barret is a playwright first, having written over twenty short and two full-length plays, most of which have had staged readings or been produced at play festivals around New England. Her three-act play, FAIR XCHANGE, was a semi-finalist in the Neil Simon Theater's new play contest in 2015.

A sometimes actor, sometimes director, she is a constant lover of the literary and performing arts. She lives with her feline companion, Fergus, on Cape Cod.